GAMBLING – A FA

Angela Willans is a freelance
was the agony aunt of *Woman's Own* for 30 years and now
handles the postal reply service for another agony aunt.
Her other books are *Conflict in Marriage, Breakaway:
Family Conflict and the Teenage Girl, Divorce and
Separation: Every Woman's Guide to a New Life* (Sheldon
Press) and *Ballads*, a novel.

Overcoming Common Problems Series

For a full list of titles please contact
Sheldon Press, Marylebone Road, London NW1 4DU

Overcoming Common Problems Series

Curing Arthritis
More ways to a drug-free life
MARGARET HILLS

Curing Illness – The Drug-Free Way
MARGARET HILLS

Depression
DR PAUL HAUCK

Divorce and Separation
Every woman's guide to a new life
ANGELA WILLANS

Don't Blame Me!
How to stop blaming yourself and other
people
TONY GOUGH

**Everything Parents Should Know About
Drugs**
SARAH LAWSON

**Family First Aid and Emergency
Handbook**
DR ANDREW STANWAY

Getting Along with People
DIANNE DOUBTFIRE

Getting the Best for Your Bad Back
DR ANTHONY CAMPBELL

Good Stress Guide, The
MARY HARTLEY

Heart Attacks – Prevent and Survive
DR TOM SMITH

Helping Children Cope with Bullying
SARAH LAWSON

Helping Children Cope with Divorce
ROSEMARY WELLS

Helping Children Cope with Grief
ROSEMARY WELLS

Hold Your Head Up High
DR PAUL HAUCK

How to Be Your Own Best Friend
DR PAUL HAUCK

How to Cope when the Going Gets Tough
DR WINDY DRYDEN AND JACK
GORDON

How to Cope with Bulimia
DR JOAN GOMEZ

How to Cope with Difficult People
ALAN HOUEL WITH CHRISTIAN
GODEFROY

How to Cope with Splitting Up
VERA PEIFFER

How to Cope with Stress
DR PETER TYRER

How to Cope with your Child's Allergies
DR PAUL CARSON

How to Do What You Want to Do
DR PAUL HAUCK

How to Improve Your Confidence
DR KENNETH HAMBLY

How to Interview and Be Interviewed
MICHELE BROWN AND GYLES
BRANDRETH

How to Keep Your Cholesterol in Check
DR ROBERT POVEY

How to Love and Be Loved
DR PAUL HAUCK

How to Pass Your Driving Test
DONALD RIDLAND

How to Stand up for Yourself
DR PAUL HAUCK

**How to Start a Conversation and Make
Friends**
DON GABOR

How to Stop Smoking
GEORGE TARGET

How to Stop Worrying
DR FRANK TALLIS

How to Survive Your Teenagers
SHEILA DAINOW

How to Untangle Your Emotional Knots
DR WINDY DRYDEN AND JACK
GORDON

How to Write a Successful CV
JOANNA GUTMANN

Hysterectomy
SUZIE HAYMAN

Is HRT Right for You?
DR ANNE MACGREGOR

The Incredible Sulk
DR WINDY DRYDEN

The Irritable Bowel Diet Book
ROSEMARY NICOL

The Irritable Bowel Stress Book
ROSEMARY NICOL

Overcoming Common Problems Series

Jealousy
DR PAUL HAUCK

Learning to Live with Multiple Sclerosis
DR ROBERT POVEY, ROBIN DOWIE
AND GILLIAN PRETT

Living Through Personal Crisis
ANN KAISER STEARNS

Living with Asthma
DR ROBERT YOUNGSON

Living with Diabetes
DR JOAN GOMEZ

Living with Grief
DR TONY LAKE

Living with High Blood Pressure
DR TOM SMITH

Making the Most of Loving
GILL COX AND SHEILA DAINOW

Making the Most of Yourself
GILL COX AND SHEILA DAINOW

Menopause
RAEWYN MACKENZIE

Migraine Diet Book, The
SUE DYSON

Motor Neurone Disease – A Family Affair
DR DAVID OLIVER

The Nervous Person's Companion
DR KENNETH HAMBLY

Overcoming Guilt
DR WINDY DRYDEN

Overcoming Stress
DR VERNON COLEMAN

The Parkinson's Disease Handbook
DR RICHARD GODWIN-AUSTEN

Sleep Like a Dream – The Drug-Free Way
ROSEMARY NICOL

Subfertility Handbook, The
VIRGINIA IRONSIDE AND SARAH BIGGS

Talking About Anorexia
How to cope with life without starving
MAROUSHKA MONRO

Talking About Miscarriage
SARAH MURPHY

Ten Steps to Positive Living
DR WINDY DRYDEN

Think Your Way to Happiness
DR WINDY DRYDEN AND JACK GORDON

Understanding Obsessions and Compulsions
A self-help manual
DR FRANK TALLIS

Understanding Your Personality
Myers-Briggs and more
PATRICIA HEDGES

A Weight Off Your Mind
How to stop worrying about your body size
SUE DYSON

When your Child Comes Out
ANNE LOVELL

You and Your Varicose Veins
DR PATRICIA GILBERT

Overcoming Common Problems

GAMBLING –
A FAMILY AFFAIR

Angela Willans

First published in Great Britain in 1996 by
Sheldon Press, SPCK, Marylebone Road, London NW1 4DU

British Library Cataloguing-in-Publication Data
A catalogue record for this book is available from the British Library
ISBN 0–85969–745–2

Photoset by Deltatype Ltd, Ellesmere Port, Cheshire
Printed in Great Britain by Biddles Ltd, Guildford and King's Lynn

Contents

Acknowledgements

I am indebted to Dr Mark Griffiths of Nottingham Trent University, whose writings and researches have proved a mine of insights and information on gambling and young people. I am also grateful to Peter Carlin of the Council for Social Concern, Air Commodore Brian Lemon of the British Casino Association, Dave Jackson of Parents of Young Gamblers and John of Gamblers Anonymous, all of whom were generous with their time and help. I owe special thanks to the many gamblers, problem gamblers, young people and parents who kindly shared their experiences with me.

Most of all, my grateful thanks are due to Paul Bellringer of the charity UK Forum on Young People and Gambling who let me draw on his vast knowledge of the gambling scene and willingly supplied answers to the many questions with which I plagued him daily.

Problem gamblers everywhere, and particularly the young, owe him a lot. His invaluable work is done on a shoestring with the constant threat of closure due to lack of funds. If any charity deserves money from the Lottery Charities Board, it is surely the UK Forum on Young People and Gambling – not only a worthy cause for the Board's patronage but a most appropriate one.

To Shirley Kennedy

1
Why do we gamble?

Everybody gambles in one way or another. It doesn't matter whether or not you approve of taking chances; this is what almost all of us are doing over and over again throughout our lives.

We are taking a risk when we make choices of any kind. The choice of something we buy is often a case of 'It's not quite what I want but I'll chance it.' Crossing the road, going on a boat or an aeroplane, driving a car, getting married, doing virtually anything except sitting at home twiddling your thumbs is taking a risk.

Where you live, what work you do, who you know, what social group you're born into can all be said to be matters of pure chance. In everyday affairs, there are references to gambling – 'nothing venture, nothing gain', 'faint heart never won fair lady', 'no pain, no gain', 'take a chance', 'nothing to lose', 'best of luck', etc. People who don't consider themselves gamblers will make wagers without even thinking about it: 'I bet it'll rain before I get home . . .', 'I bet the phone will go as soon as I get in the shower . . .', 'I bet you £1 Peter's left his lunch-box behind again.' When we say these things, we mean more than simply 'I *expect* it will rain.' We mean 'I'm so convinced it will rain that I'm willing to wager on it.'

The gambling instinct can be seen in children quite early on. They like games where you can play for winnings, even if it's only matchsticks or Monopoly money. The hotheads who play 'last across the road is a chicken' take the biggest gamble of all – and so do the 'joyriders'.

Even raffles are deemed dangerous enough to be banned in some countries, which decidedly puts them in the gambling category. However, neither these nor lotteries are likely to cause serious addictions. The real enthusiasts, who are likely to go on to become regular or even compulsive gamblers, can be recognized by their willingness to bet on anything – from two flies crawling up a wall (50p says the right-hand one will win) to future movements of the money markets (five million dollars say the Share Index will go up).

So gambling is in our bones – but not, in fact, as much in female bones as in male ones. This is no surprise when we consider that risk-taking – the essence of gambling – is undoubtedly a male trait, and keeping things safe, secure and 'the same' – the antithesis of gambling – is predominantly a female one. That's partly why, in this book, I use *he* much more than *she* when writing about a problem gambler, because male gamblers are in the majority and problem male gamblers even more so.

However, in most contexts, like here when we're talking about why people gamble, I use *he* for convenience to mean *she* as well. When I'm clearly referring specifically to a male or female then *he* or *she* will mean what it says. There's more in Chapter 3 about gender differences in gambling behaviour.

Another spur to gambling which is part of most people's nature is the belief in superstition, fate, luck or kismet. 'Luck be a lady tonight' sings the craps player in *Guys and Dolls* on the gambler's principle that a winner is favoured by luck and a loser isn't. Either way, the gambler believes the outcome of the craps game is nothing to do with him or anything he does or doesn't do – it's all down to luck, good or bad.

In everyday life, this idea of luck or fate overtakes reality and makes us behave in mildly superstitious ways. How often have you thought 'If I take my umbrella, it won't rain'? This works on the principle that, if we anticipate unpleasant events and work out what we'd do if they happened, we can actually ward them off. From this we can see that what is often happening in gambling is both an appeal to chance or luck and also an attempt to control the workings of chance.

A divorced woman used to go regularly to bingo sessions. 'After a while I didn't like bingo because someone else chooses the numbers,' she said. She switched to roulette where she chose the numbers and could feel in control. Since she is now a gambling addict, it's clear that in her case this control doesn't extend to limiting the amount of gambling, only to how it's done.

People who fail to take responsibility for themselves – losers, drop-outs, druggies, drunks and persistent criminals – are the most extreme examples of basing one's life on the principle of luck. They will always blame their problems on something 'out there' – their parents, their background, their treatment as a child, the ill will of other people, the government, etc. They feel that they personally have nothing to do with all the bad fortune that befalls them and that luck reigns supreme.

In fact, they have a right to feel resentful of parents and others who failed to help them develop a sense of their own worth and of the power they could have over their own destinies. This is the touchstone of the confident, creative adult – the ability to direct your life according to the best interests of yourself and of the people around you and the recognition that when you take chances it is you and no one else who makes that choice and who must accept the consequences. It is all based on self-esteem – and that, as we shall see, is what the problem gambler lacks.

There is, of course, a big difference between taking chances in everyday life and gambling for recreation. When we gamble we consciously choose to exchange something of value – usually money – for the chance of winning something of greater value – usually more money. This is normally what starts someone on their first taste of gambling. After that other motives join this one and, in some cases, overshadow it. The reasons why most people gamble, and why beginner gamblers turn into regulars, are:

- Money.
- Social life.
- A remedy for boredom.
- The 'buzz'.

Money

The main *initial* trigger for the new gambler is the desire, and sometimes desperation, for profit. For the really poor, gambling is disastrously seen as a way out of their debt or difficulties, and getting a big win becomes more and more important as they go on.

In fact, in all the countries with a gambling culture, it's the poorest people who, in proportion to their income, spend the most on pools, lotteries and scratch cards. If they don't win, it's a spur to go on until they do (nobody really entertains the idea that they might never win anything) and if they do win, it's a spur to go on until they win some more. Mandy, who's a 24-year-old single parent, explains how this happens.

Darren and Amy aren't at school yet so I can't work. Their dad went off before Amy was even born. The Child Support people can't find him – no one can – so I'm living on benefit at the moment. All I get is £110 and I can't see it getting any better, not even when I can get a job. There's nothing to look forward to so what can I do but go for the big win? I spend £5 every week on the scratch cards and £2 on the Lottery. I just know it's going to come good some time so I can't stop – it would be just my luck for my number to come up the very week I don't buy a card.

I know it's a lot out of my benefit but why shouldn't I spend it on what I want, for me and the kids and our future? My mother doesn't

3

agree with me spending so much on a gamble but she and Dad go for eight lines on the Lottery between them, so she can't talk. They've won several tenners. And Mum's very good at giving me a fiver now and then. It's a struggle sometimes but the kids don't ever go short of food or anything important. It gives me something to get excited about on Saturday nights too. So why not?

Some forms of gambling need money to start with, your own or somebody else's, for example, gambling on the stock market, or playing at expensive, up-market casinos like the ones in Monte Carlo or Las Vegas.

These high-stakes gamblers are slightly different from the average punter who gambles in the hope of a profit. They may appear to be interested only in becoming fabulously rich but in reality, as the pattern of their gambling shows, it isn't this that drives them on to stake more and more. Risk-taking is the name of the game and this type of gambler will quickly get into a fantasy world where he scarcely realizes what enormous sums of money – usually not his own – he's staking on the outside chance of making a huge killing.

He blithely goes on, chasing one enormous loss with another, his hope of a gigantic profit gradually giving way to a state of panic. At that stage, he would gladly settle for merely recouping his losses, but is drawn into wilder and wilder gambles until he's heavily into personal debt or, as in the case of Nick Leeson and the collapse of Barings Bank in 1995, until the source of the stake money has completely dried up. Then all he can do is head for the hills.

Donald illustrates this type of gambler and his motivation. He is a dignified, grandfatherly figure who lives in a tiny bedsitter on a state pension and a small family hand-out. He used to live with his daughter and her family in a big country house in the Surrey stockbroker belt and was comfortably off, with a good private pension, considerable savings and no money worries. His wife had died several years before he showed any interest in gambling. 'Thank goodness she can't see me now,' he says.

You'll never believe this but it all started with BT shares when the telephones were privatized. I thought it was wonderful when I made such a good, quick profit. I went on to buy other national issues and eventually I got the shares bug and was into speculating in a big way. From being just a retired civil servant I turned into a somebody, a winner, a clever chap who had luck on his side. I was never short of drinking pals who thought I was a financial wizard.

I put thousands of pounds into a company who were getting backers for some oil exploration. I wanted them to find oil so badly that I began to pray for it night and day. I could think of nothing else. Well, they didn't find oil and I lost my thousands so I started gambling with other shares to get back to square one.

I had to borrow money wherever I could – by now my daughter and her husband had washed their hands of me. I sold them my share of the house and moved out. I miss the family terribly. When the loans from friends stopped coming (I couldn't ever pay any of them back – they were gifts, not loans and they knew it) I had to gamble on credit. But then I lost more thousands on the Stock Exchange and, of course, my credit ran out. I owed the bookmakers everything I possessed and a lot more.

At last, I'd learned my lesson. I went to Gamblers Anonymous. I felt really bad at first. I was looking at myself for the first time and I thought 'You blithering idiot – what have you done to yourself?' But it began to get better after a few meetings – it was such a relief to get all that stupidity off my chest. Since then, although it's been hell trying to get straight financially, I've really found out who I am. I can have a laugh now and enjoy people's company. I feel free somehow, and more human.

Social life

Most forms of gambling involve the company of other gamblers – in the arcade or the betting-shop, at the track, in the bingo hall, or in the casino. This is a strong pull for the secret gambler or the one whose family and friends all disapprove of his hobby. Here, he's with people who understand him and like being in his company. This is where his real friends are and where he can be at ease.

Roddy is a recovering compulsive gambler whose favourite haunt was a local casino.

It was marvellous there. I was always in the doghouse at home – as soon as I made to go out I was niggled at – (*he puts on a high voice*) 'Where are you going? If it's the casino again, you needn't bother coming back. You haven't got any money on you, have you? Where did you get it? Did you pay the TV licence. . . ?'

And on and on it went. Like as not, I hadn't paid the TV licence, or the electricity or anything else. It would be lying there in my wallet, all ready to get those darling chips and start on the roller-coaster to –

well, what? That was the lovely thing – you didn't know whether it was going to be win or lose. A wonderful feeling of anticipation. And all my pals would be there – you could see the relief and liberation in their faces – some of them, like me, had come out with nagging ringing in their ears. We'd swap notes – how's it going today? – and have a drink at the bar. Then we'd huddle round the tables – they had lovely lighting there, very warm and cheerful.

Everyone made you feel welcome. It was dead opposite to the atmosphere at home. There, when I slunk back, there was either dead silence and everyone asleep or she'd be sitting up with some new account of my sins – 'Your father rang and asked when you were going to pay him back. How much? *How bloody much*? Haven't you got any feelings left for *anybody. . .*?' Well, I hadn't really. All I knew was that I wanted to be miles away from my family and just spend all my time in that place where I was really happy and where people were pleased to see me.

The opportunity to be involved with others and the feeling of belonging is so important that a gambler can get as hooked on the social element as on the chance of winning, just as someone can become as addicted to the company at the local as to the alcohol he drinks there.

A remedy for boredom

The regular gambler doesn't usually have much to look forward to except the times when he's actually gambling. The problem gambler has nothing else to look forward to – gambling is his whole life. That's one of the reasons why he's taken up gambling in the first place – his life was without any comparable interest or stimulation.

Even when he's not gambling, he can spread his interest widely over the rest of his day – he can read about the sport he bets on, work out the odds, study the form, tinker about with card and roulette systems, maybe go and have a 'junior' gamble on the pub fruit machine – it all serves to keep boredom at bay if there's nothing else going for you.

Many young gamblers say they gamble simply because it gives them 'something to do'. Some had fathers who found it a good way to pass the time and, in a fatherly sort of way, they thought it might do the same for their sons.

At 11, Tom was already a smart card-player. Like many keen gamblers, he'd caught the bug from his father who used to come home boasting of his triumphs at pontoon in the lunch-hour at work. He had, of course, kept quiet about the losing games. Soon Tom was a welcome player at the kitchen table in the evenings, when his father's workmates used to drift in with some cans of beer and a small amount of £1 coins. After a while, he was winning all the time and not so popular. By the time his father's group had graduated to whisky and £5 notes, Tom was 18 and had moved on to casinos, where pontoon was known as blackjack, stakes could be anything from 25p to £100,000 and the gambling could get really serious.

I was working in a big mail-order firm. It wasn't tightly managed in those days and we were never really stretched. It was dead boring. I used to find a game somewhere during the day – my lunch-hour became pretty elastic and nobody seemed to be bothered. It was in the evenings, though, that I really got going. I would go to the casino every night it was open, and stay till it closed at four in the morning. Some people went there for the social bit – they used to spend a lot of the time drinking. But I gave that a miss – it would have interfered with my concentration. The thing is that I simply came alive at the tables – I wasn't bored or depressed. In comparison, the rest of my life was like a dull, grey, rainy day.

The buzz

This – the thrill of taking a chance – is what takes a gambler closest to the brink of addiction. You can see young men playing the fruit machines getting hyped up by the flashing lights and sounds, thumping the buttons, punching the air with their fists and hunching over the machine with such staring-eyed concentration that they appear almost hypnotized.

Tests on a gambler at a casino have shown that while he's waiting for the roulette wheel to slow down and is at the peak of tension, wondering whether he's going to win or lose, he actually experiences certain physical changes such as raised blood pressure, a slowing-down of the digestive system, a surge of adrenalin and an increased heart rate. This last change is particularly striking. The average resting heartbeat is 72 per minute. The roulette player waiting for the spin had a heartbeat of 162 per minute. This suggests that you can get on a physical 'high' with gambling in much the same way as people do on alcohol or drugs.

A 50-year-old man who gambled away his home, job and marriage describes the thrill he got from betting on the horses.

For me the excitement was in the risk, nothing else. Unless I was staking more than I could afford there wasn't any buzz. Of course, you have to wait between races and that's when the tension starts up and gets you really excited. It's a terrific let-down when you don't win. You come down with such a crash that you can feel really angry and fed up. But you never wish you hadn't had the bet. You forget almost at once about losing the money – you just want to get back to that excited state again as fast as you can.

These people's stories explain some of the needs that are met by taking part in gambling. However, although all gamblers probably start off hoping that one or more of these needs will be met, we don't all get drawn into gambling at the same frequency or into the same types of gambling. Nor are we all equally in danger of becoming compulsive or problem gamblers. There are five types of gambler, each with its own risk of addiction.

Types of gambler

Occasional

People who have a bet only on special events like the Boat Race, the Grand National or the Eurovision Song Contest. They are very unlikely to become compulsive gamblers.

Regular

People who gamble every week on the lottery, buy scratch cards every week, go to the betting shop or casino a few days a week, or regularly play fruit machines. Regular gambling can easily become compulsive gambling.

Serious

The serious gambler may be in a syndicate for doing the pools or the Lottery or he may simply have a system of his own for maximizing his chances of winning. Most serious gamblers methodically work out the odds, whatever their favourite type of gambling is, and are likely to study form when it comes to horse and dog racing. Because they are close to having an obsessive attitude to gambling, they are at great risk of becoming addicted.

Professional

People who gamble on the stock market are termed professional because they are working with inside knowledge and have to use a large degree of skill and nerve to take chances on the movement of share prices and value of stock, etc. Some gamblers who go to all the race meetings and also work on inside knowledge become professional by virtue of the fact that they make some sort of a living out of gambling.

Many players on the financial markets are young, reckless and new to the possibility of making vast fortunes; some others are mature but greedy. Both types have a high risk of going on and on with bigger and bigger stakes until the whole house of cards comes tumbling down. But your true professional gambler – on the stock market, at the races or in the casino – is cool and wise and seldom comes to a sticky end. He doesn't make a fortune either, it must be said.

Compulsive

For the compulsive gambler, gambling replaces all other interests. He can't stop and doesn't want to stop. He thinks he has a charmed life and will win in the end. He is physically and emotionally dependent on the 'buzz' he gets from gambling. He is an addict and needs help.

Chapter 3 tells you how to recognize a gambling addict, Chapter 5 how to cope with him, Chapter 6 about help and Chapter 7 about recovery.

2

The gambling scene

Who gambles?

A watershed in the UK's gambling scene was reached on 14 November 1995. This was the day that the National Lottery was launched and almost instantly it brought about enormous changes in the who, how, what and when of gambling in the UK.

In the pre-lottery days, 74 per cent of the population took part in gambling activities. After the Lottery started, the figure shot up to 90 per cent and has stayed there. Up to 1994, gambling had been a predominantly male pastime and the typical gambler was a skilled manual worker aged between 35 and 44 whose bets went on the horses or pools. The Lottery has changed that picture dramatically and drawn into regular gambling more women in all age groups, more people aged 16–24 (although this is the least enthusiastic group) and more people aged 55 and over. However, from the point of view of social class, it's still the skilled manual workers and their families who are the keenest players.

Compulsive gamblers have always been part of the gambling scene – it's estimated that 1 million to 1.5 million adult gamblers qualify as having a problem, which means they're out of control, betting more than they can afford and on the downhill slide to disaster. Gamblers Anonymous (GA), the organization for gamblers who seriously want to stop, are approached by 15,000 people per year. In the first year of the Lottery, calls to GA rose by 17 per cent. However, GA does not claim that this increase is attributable to the Lottery and there can be no evidence that it is or isn't.

What we do know for sure is that the UK is now a gambling nation and that 'having a flutter' – never a minority interest, it's true, but hardly in the forefront of national life – is now an extremely popular activity and is even the highlight of many people's lives. This means that gambling is now truly a family affair. In most households in the country, father or mother or both will be buying lottery tickets or scratch cards, going fairly regularly to the betting shop, bingo hall, horse- or dog-racing track, doing the pools or visiting a casino.

Their over-18-year-old children will be buying scratch cards or lottery tickets and playing the fruit machines in pubs, chip shops and cafés. The younger children are playing the fruit machines and video games in the arcades or spending their pocket money on scratch cards.

Even grandad and grandma may be scrimping on food in order to buy a stake in the Lottery. There is no limit on the age, gender, income or educational standing of the people for whom the Lottery jackpot seems to promise a miraculous sea change in their lives, a chance to 'get away from it all' and start afresh with every dream made real. As we shall see later in this chapter, the National Lottery – from here on called simply the Lottery – has revolutionized the UK's gambling habits. For a start, 21 per cent of the people who buy tickets *had never gambled before*.

Background

Since gambling is part of human nature, it crops up in one form or another in every country and culture throughout the world and has done since the early Greek and Roman civilizations. It's said that Caesar invaded Gaul in order to pay his gambling debts, and the first recorded public lotteries took place in Augustus Caesar's reign. Gambling is even mentioned in the Bible, when St John describes how soldiers at the cross cast lots for Christ's clothes.

At first, it was betting on games with dice or bones. Then, around the fifteenth century, playing-cards came on the scene and there was gambling on all kinds of sports like wrestling, cock-fighting and horse-racing. By the eighteenth century there were clubs in London, like Crockfords, Whites and Brooks, where gentlemen could gamble away their fortunes on the cards, and next came the casinos – again a gambling venue at first restricted to 'gentlemen'.

There followed a host of ways in which people could spend their money in the hope of getting something back – from gambling on newer and ever-increasing forms of sport and racing to raffles, sweepstakes, bingo, board-games, card-games, dice games, fairground games, and one-armed bandits.

In descending order of popularity, the types of gambling enjoyed in the UK today are:

- National Lottery and scratch cards
- football pools
- other lotteries and raffles
- fruit machines in pubs
- bingo
- horse-racing

• casino gambling.

Which is the best bet for a big win?

If you set out to win a large sum in a single gambling session, you'd have to find the best method, as well as the best odds, for maximizing your chances. A bookmaking firm has worked this out for you and it turns out that your best bet would be a £1 chip on one roulette number, with a win riding over three more winning spins; next best is £10 on five winning horses at odds of 9–1; next would be a game of blackjack (pontoon), although you'd have to beat the bank 18 times in a row and let your wins ride.

Scratch cards come next with a 2.57 million to one chance of winning £50,000. It would be almost impossible, or would take a very long time, to win a large sum on a fruit machine. Most have a top prize of £6 and you're facing odds of 40–1 against winning that. Football pools, offering a 7.5 million–1 chance of winning a £2 million jackpot, are a better bet than the Lottery – but then so is almost everything. Set out in order of your chances of making a million, the different forms of gambling look like this:

• roulette – a casino game
• horse-racing
• blackjack – another casino game
• pools
• scratch cards
• the Lottery
• fruit machine.

The Lottery has the lowest stake but the longest odds – 14.5 million against winning the jackpot. It's been estimated that you have a greater chance of being mugged, losing your job and having your house repossessed *on the same day* than of winning the jackpot – and also a greater chance of dying tomorrow. Another way of putting it is that there's more chance of Elvis Presley landing a UFO on top of the Loch Ness monster . . .

Rules and regulations

Gambling has always attracted criminals of all kinds, from cheats, fraudsters and petty crooks to large-scale swindlers. Minor frauds associated with gambling include marked cards, loaded dice, false deals, false postmarks, tapped phones, rigged equipment, etc.

In the US, in the 1920s and 30s, gambling was tied up with well-known gangsters and mobsters like Al Capone, who, backed up by machine-guns and hordes of sharp-suited supporters, was running breweries, brothels, protection rackets and gambling dens all over Chicago. He and an opposing gang-leader, 'Bugs' Moran, opened rival dog-racing tracks with a heavy emphasis on betting facilities. Some of the most popular films about gambling, like *The Sting*, involving bets on horse-racing, and *Cincinnati Kid*, about poker, illustrate the powerful emotions at work in the keen gambler, so powerful that many gamblers lost their lives for being on the wrong side of a struggle for profits.

From the start there were restrictions on gambling – the Greeks were punished for betting on dice games because gambling was considered a threat to state organization – and most countries now have laws to limit gambling venues, the age at which people can gamble, and when and for how long they can gamble.

In the UK, most of the laws on gambling date from the years between 1661 and 1960. Common objections to gambling through the ages were mostly based on an extremely class-conscious view of gambling's drawbacks, rather like nineteenth-century attitudes to alcohol: i.e. it was good for gentlemen, but bad for women and the working class. The case against gambling was:

- it 'weakened' the gambler
- it caused hardship to his dependants
- it inconvenienced the state
- criminals made money at it
- why should the lower orders enjoy it?

Strangely, there are many countries which frown on gambling but allow state lotteries. This may have something to do with the large revenues raised for the government and for good causes – including causes previously funded by the government out of taxes. Indeed it would be hard to think of any other reason for the introduction of a national lottery except for raising money for the government as well as for other beneficiaries. The one in the UK is often not unreasonably described as another form of tax. The government gets 12p for every £1 spent on tickets or scratch cards – easily the lion's share of the spoils.

Is gambling bad for you?

It's not only or even mainly to keep out the criminals that laws were brought in to restrict gambling. It was also because governments, church leaders, moralists and social observers have tended to disagree about whether gambling is harmful or not and so governments are unable to decide where to draw the line. Until recently, however, they seemed to think that the line ought to be drawn somewhere.

The dark history of fruit-machine gambling and its young addicts (see Chapter 8) clearly shows the concerns about addiction on the one hand and the dismissive attitude of government on the other. In between were most people, who didn't give much thought to the effects of gambling and had no views on it.

The only people who knew how deadly the habit could be when it became obsessive were the compulsive gamblers themselves, their partners and families, the people who helped them and some church bodies, social workers and academics who had studied the subject or were otherwise involved. In the opposite corner were, and still are, the people who are obliged to think about the gambling industry because they are helping to increase its profits and widen its attractions, and who are convinced that it can never be harmful.

In a way, they speak the truth. Gambling is not harmful in itself. It's a very enjoyable activity and no one wants to ban it. It does, however, do great harm to people who cannot control their betting – and to their nearest and dearest. In Chapter 3 we'll see what features of the gambling experience lead to addiction and what kind of person is most likely to become addicted.

I'll also leave for later in this chapter a look at how the Lottery has changed the UK and what difference it's made to the lives of those who live there. For now, we'll note that it has all the necessary features to bring old hands and new recruits into its gambling net and to hold them there, and its scratch cards, with their easy access and quick fix, have a particular appeal to the young *and are highly addictive.*

The irony of this situation is that, far from laws on gambling being tightened up since the Lottery floodgates were opened, the UK government has ever since been busy relaxing them so that all the other forms of gambling which were beginning to lose out would have a fairer slice of the action. So what's the state of play for the other forms of gambling in the UK?

Forms of gambling

Casinos

Gaming in casinos used to be restricted to the rich and stylish who could afford either to fly over to Deauville, the Riviera or Monte Carlo or to join in the games held by up-market gamblers in luxurious private houses in Britain. After a famous case in 1958 when John Aspinall, his mother and a friend were prosecuted for playing *chemin de fer* in a London flat – ending in the judge's direction that there was no case to answer – the law was revised to make gaming legal only in recognized premises.

It was then that casinos began to spring up in the UK and during the 1960s, when there were few controls, there were over 1,200 of them. Gradually, new rules were introduced until casinos in this country became more strictly regulated than in any other and now number about 120. They are essentially clubs, open to members only, with various restrictions on membership including a ban on under-18s. Throughout 1995 casinos suffered so badly from unfair competition with the far less regulated Lottery and its seductive advertising – casinos were not even allowed to have their details in the Yellow Pages – that the government started consultations with the gaming industry early in 1996. The result will almost certainly be a considerable relaxation of the restrictions on the way casinos are run.

All in all, casinos have a much more homely image than they used to and, because women feel safe and secure in them and no one is allowed to behave badly there, they can truly be called places for adult 'family' entertainment.

All the same casinos have a small quota of problem gamblers. 'It's reckoned that 2 per cent of the whole gambling population are problem gamblers,' says the General Secretary of the British Casino Association, 'and we estimate that we get only about 2 per cent of them. The last thing a casino wants is someone who's not gaming within their means. They might throw money at us but it's soon gone and that gives us a very short relationship with the member instead of the long one that we'd like. When it crops up, we deal with the problem on an individual basis.'

Gaming machines

There are three types:
- *AWP or Amusement with Prize machines*, commonly known as fruit machines because of the pictures of fruit which spin round on reels. These are found in pubs, cafés, amusement arcades, motorway service areas, etc. and are legal for players of any age. Arcade owners, however, have their own rules whereby children under 16 are banned from inland arcades at all times and from seaside arcades during school hours.

   There are an estimated 230,000 AWP machines throughout the

UK. A sidelight on the value-for-money aspect of these machines is that the reels all come to rest after five seconds. With a stake of 20p you are therefore paying for your pleasure at a rate of £2.40 per minute which, even allowing for the occasional win, sounds like good news for the fruit-machine owners.

- *Jackpot machines* (with a bigger stake and bigger prizes) can only be sited in registered clubs with a gaming licence. No one under 18 is allowed entry.
- *Electronic and computer games* – the video and computer games children play at home and in arcades. They are not gambling or gaming machines in the sense that you can win prizes or cash playing them, but they are giving rise to the same kind of concern about compulsive playing as traditional forms of gambling.

A lot of concerned experts have studied these games and their players. I tell you about what they have found out in Chapter 8 on young gamblers.

Horse-racing and dog-racing

The first recorded horse race in England was run in 210 AD. Not recorded is whether there were wagers on the winner but I would place a heavy bet on the chance that there were. Although greyhound owners have always put their dogs up as challengers in races against other dogs – and doubtless had money or a round of drinks on the outcome – it wasn't until 1926 that the first public greyhound racing event in the UK took place at Belle Vue, Manchester.

Before long the government of the day began attempting to control gaming and gambling – and harvest some of the large sums of money finding their way into the pockets of the bookies, the tote and the casino owners. A tax on betting was introduced in 1926, abolished in 1929 and introduced again in 1967. Currently, the total revenue from gaming and gambling taken by the UK government is around £1,114,000,000.

Except for the weekly mega-wins on the Lottery and other big wins on the pools, at the casino or on the races, punters rarely cover their stake money. One card-player reckoned his only chance of winning was 'to play snap with a man who stutters'. (And it's said that the only way to come out of a casino with a million pounds is to go in with two million.)

By 1960 the betting laws were in a mess and class-wise highly discriminatory. The well-off were able to gamble freely off-course via telephone credit accounts with their bookmakers. Joe Public, however, with no bank account and no classy references, would have had a very dusty answer from any bookmaker, even supposing he'd had the temerity to ask for credit in the first place.

As any other form of bookmaking was illegal – there were no betting offices then – the ordinary middle-class or working-class punter had to play a furtive game with the street bookmakers by placing his bets with the bookies' runners. The runners, for their part, hung around street corners with an eye open both for their regular customers and also for the police, or set up temporary shop in garages, warehouses, pubs and doorways.

Old hands say that, because there was an added risk involved – Would they get caught by 'the law'? Would they be able to get their bet on before the off? – there was much more of a buzz about this illegal betting than about the lawful kind in betting-shops – though everyone agrees that on-course gambling, if you can get there, is the best of all.

In 1960 bookmaking at last became legal and by the 1980s there were 12,000 or so betting-shops in the UK. The lowest age for admission to a betting-shop is 18. Bookies' fortunes took a downturn with the advent of the Lottery and the big bookmaking firms took another when horse-racing on Sundays was allowed for the first time in the summer of 1995, thus taking money away from the chain betting-shops.

Pools

Football pools are so called because they are a type of 'pool betting'. Players forecast the number of draws in a list of matches and all their stakes are pooled. Money is deducted to cover the firm's overheads, tax liabilities and profits and the rest is shared among the winners, i.e. the players whose forecasts turn out to be right.

In the UK, pools betting is limited to over-16s and is second in popularity to the Lottery and scratch cards, attracting over two million punters in the winter and not a lot fewer in the summer. Like the Lottery it has small stakes and big prizes and the waiting time between the bet and the result, whilst being nothing like instant, is under a week and therefore not as long as some raffles and sweepstakes and about the same waiting time as the Lottery.

The image of pools gambling is of the family sitting round the kitchen table all pitching in with their suggestions of how to forecast the draws, or a group of people in the workplace clubbing together to bet on several chances. Certainly, it has none of the glamour and glitz of its close rival but none of the dangers either. There may be pools addicts but no one I know has ever come across one. Clearly, they either keep a low profile or they're an endangered species.

Unfortunately, pools firms have also been losing out since the Lottery started. One pools firm claims that business has fallen by 15 per cent and there was a further downturn when the scratch cards came in. They were not allowed to advertise before the Lottery but now they can.

Bingo

Bingo is the only form of gambling where, up to now, women have outnumbered men – of its 2.8 million regular players, 83 per cent are women. It's easy to see why. It's cheap and cheerful and is the ideal form of gambling if you want a night out with friends or some good company if you live alone. In fact, it's the answer to all four of the motives for gambling described in Chapter 1 – profit, social life, relief of boredom and 'the buzz'.

Bingo playing is currently almost as severely regulated as casino gaming, being restricted to members only – who must be over 18 – in licensed clubs, with various limits on prizes, and no advertising.

Although half a million people per day gamble in the UK's 970 bingo clubs – staking in total more than £800 million a year – the bingo industry, like every other form of gambling, is said to have suffered from the impact of the Lottery. As a result, moves are being made to ease most of the restrictions, making it possible for anyone to join a game of bingo as easily as they buy a lottery ticket or scratch card.

Lotteries

Lotteries are 400 years old. The oldest one started in Italy in the sixteenth century. The famous Numbers Game, illegally run by bootleggers in the 1930s in the US, was a form of lottery. Bingo is derived from it and used to be called by the Italian word for lottery, which is *lotto*. Most European countries have lotteries – Spain has several national and local lotteries and has recorded the biggest win ever – the equivalent of £180 million in the first week of 1996. In the UK anyone wanting to run one has to have a licence.

The Lottery

Until 14 November 1994, the word 'lottery' probably evoked an image for most people of village halls and church fund-raising – or perhaps of excitable Spaniards kissing each other in hysterical celebration. Now it's a word that draws three million people to their local newsagents or superstore to spend £1 or more on the one in 14.5 million chance of winning £8 million-plus, or on a likelier chance of winning smaller sums on the scratch cards. It means the £1 million profit that Camelot, the Lottery operators, are said to make *every week* and the £600 million that went to the Treasury in the first year of its operation. It means, in fact, the biggest lottery in the world, beating even the famous, long-established lotteries of Spain, France and Texas.

The money involved is mind-boggling. The sale of Lottery tickets, together with scratch cards, which came into play in March 1995, amounts to more than £90 million a week or about £4.5 billion a year, which is the equivalent of the entire national income of a country like Panama or Paraguay. The average family spends £2.43 a week on numbers and scratch cards – more than it spends on bread, books or cake in a week.

The Lottery also means 'loadsa' money for 'good causes', not all of which the general public thinks either 'good' or particularly in need of a hand-out. In fact, a survey done at the end of the Lottery's first year of operation showed that players were under the impression that much more of the proceeds went to good causes than actually does. It emerged that most people would like to have more of a say in where the money goes – which is not very realistic – and also favour some of the millions of pounds of prize money being diverted to charities and medical research – a very reasonable and realistic hope.

The biggest effect on the nation, which is a lasting one, was that we all had a lot of fun dreaming about winning the jackpot and asking each other 'What would you do if you won?' We also had a warm feeling that we were doing some people a lot of good by 'donating' our money to the Lottery and we didn't feel a bit like *real* gamblers who might go over the top and get out of control.

One of the interesting things that emerged from sharing jackpot fantasies with each other is that winning a lot of money doesn't seem to be so much about being rich as about having power and freedom. It gives you the means to do your own things, go your own way, make your own choices, be generous to the people you love or who you believe deserve your charity and dismiss the people you don't like but up to now have had to rub along with.

The vista of tropical holidays, luxury cars, large homes and lots of leisure time seem to pale beside the delights of walking out of a job you're fed up with, moving away from a run-down neighbourhood, turning the roof-space into a spare bedroom, being able to pay bills without a care and never having to worry about how you'd cope with poor health or old age.

See if the following fantasies are anything like yours. A self-employed accountant with three school-age children:

I'd invest a lot to pay for all the kids to go to private schools where they had small classes and things like music teaching, language labs and a lot of sport facilities. I'd keep working just to have something to do and not to let my clients down but I'd make sure my wife never had to go out to work again (unless she really wanted to) and I'd buy her a brand-new fitted kitchen. We wouldn't move because we like it here, but, if I could get permission, I'd build on an extension and a conservatory.

A widowed office cleaner, aged 41:

If I won, my bosses wouldn't see me for dust. It used to be a lovely firm to work for. There were a dozen of us sent out to work as a team in different buildings. We all loved it – it was such fun – we took turns making the tea and bringing something special for breakfast.

But now it's been taken over by a couple of young manager-types, you know – all smart suits and slicked back hair and calling you 'dear' – what a cheek – and we're sent all over the place on our own or in twos, and all for less money. I'd love to pack it in. We all would. It's enough to make you howl, remembering how it was and how happy we were. But what can I do? What can any of us do? We've all got rent to pay and mouths to feed. Just a bit more money – not even the jackpot, and I could tell those idiots to stuff their job. No – it had better be the jackpot and then all the other girls can do the same.

A divorced woman doing secretarial work from home:

I wouldn't want a cruise or a big house or anything like that. I'd give my two children enough to pay off their mortgages and I'd settle a sum on my three grandchildren – to have until they were older, not to spend. I'd have my home decorated and, as my present car is falling to bits I'd get another a bit newer but the same make.

I'd go on working but having some money would mean that I could pick and choose who I work for. Most of my customers are dears but some of them are pigs and I'd drop those. I know a lot of neighbours who are poorly or disabled – I'd give them what they needed –

enough here for an electric wheelchair, a bit there for a stair-lift. I think this is better than giving it to charity – it's often needed closer to home. I wouldn't like the publicity at all. I'd rather do things secretly and surprise people.

We can all be forgiven for letting rip with our fantasies, especially as most of our dreams are so well-disposed towards our families and friends. The huge odds against winning, which should put us off, are wonderfully disguised by the tremendous hype surrounding the Lottery. 'It could be you' is the message, put across on TV in a swirl of gold and whoops of joy. There are, of course, more chances of winning smaller prizes, especially the £10 for three winning numbers. But the fact that all the other lotteries in the country have suffered from the National Lottery's popularity shows that smaller prizes aren't enough to draw the punters – it's the big one we're all after.

Not long after the scratch cards were launched in March 1995 the first doubts appeared about 'gambling fever' and the harm it seemed to be doing. There were more and more protests about the Lottery's encouragement to 'greed, false hopes and overindulgence'. The huge amounts gambled on the Lottery and scratch cards were said to be unbalancing the nation's economy in the same way that they unbalanced the punters' budgets. There were more and more tales of woe about the effects of the Lottery – job losses at pools firms, betting-shops and bookmaking firms, charities falling by the wayside, winners falling out with family and friends over claims to a share of the winnings, anger at the enormous profits of Camelot and at some of the recipients of lottery money.

Agony aunt Marje Proops OBE, who was a member of the Royal Commission on Gambling in 1978, now regrets that the final report came out in favour of a national lottery. 'I wish we'd said "no",' she says now.

I'm not against gambling or the Lottery. But I'm appalled at the way it's run. We concluded on the Commission that a national lottery would be a good idea but on condition that the top prize was £500,000, that there were more small prizes than we get now, that much more money went to good causes and that it should be a non-commercial venture run by the Gaming Board who would extract a modest profit.

What we didn't bargain for was the operators stuffing their back-pockets with huge wads of crinklies. And 5.5 pence in the £1 to charity isn't enough, not when the top prize is an obscene eight million or more. Also, the way that women have been drawn into gambling is a worry – before their interest in it was mainly social, as in bingo. But now more and more of them could get addicted and I'm hearing all the time from women going mad on the scratch cards and getting into terrible debt to loan sharks, etc. I'd ban scratch cards – much too tempting and dangerous.

I'll be referring to the Lottery and scratch cards again throughout the book – their influence has endless ramifications – but for hints on how to keep this and other forms of gambling under control see Chapter 11 on safe gambling.

3

When is gambling a problem?

Throughout this book, and particularly in this chapter, I'll refer to the gambler who's out of control as an addicted gambler, compulsive gambler, or problem gambler. This is because all the literature and all the experts on the subject seem to have their favourite term for this type of gambler. They all mean the same thing. Problem gambler is my favourite.

The gambling man

Another point to clear up is the use of *he* for the problem gambler. As I said in Chapter 1, I'll be using *he*, and not *she*, nearly all the time in this book and this needs some further explanation. As we saw in the last chapter, gambling used to be a man's game, except for bingo which has always had a strong social element that appealed to women. We already know, however, that since the arrival of the Lottery and scratch cards many more women have been drawn into gambling, mostly because of the opportunity to share their dreams about what they'd do with a big win and also because the outlets for a bet are where they do their daily or weekly shopping.

The reason that I'm not talking about *her*, the problem gambler as much as *him*, the problem gambler, is because the fact that there are now more women and girls gambling than there used to be is about *all* we know. We don't know how many female gamblers there are, or how many are addicted. All that's known for sure is that, apart from bingo, the lottery and scratch cards, ways of having a flutter attract far more men than women. Women are outnumbered by men at casinos, on fruit machines, in betting-shops and at the dogs and horses.

What is also known is that far fewer female gamblers become addicted, and far fewer of those who do become addicted seek help. There are interesting reasons suggested for this reluctance to get help – I have a look at them in Chapter 6. We can also look out for a change in the gender picture before long. We know from personal stories on television that many women living alone or on the poverty line are spending a large part of their low incomes on scratch cards and cannot stop themselves. That's addiction.

What is gambling addiction?

Man or woman, are you in any danger of becoming addicted if you have the occasional bet? Well, you don't even merit the label 'gambler' if all you do is have the odd flutter. Buying a raffle ticket now and then, say, or having a bet on the General Election results, makes you merely 'someone who sometimes gambles'. You are no more at risk of becoming a real gambler, or of becoming addicted to gambling, than someone who has the occasional cigarette is called a smoker, or is at risk of becoming a tobacco addict.

An addicted gambler is something else. There are several different theories about what that 'something else' is. Some say the problem gambler is a sick man and his habit is a psychiatric illness. Its symptoms are:

- loss of control
- extremes of emotion
- withdrawal symptoms when not gambling.

This theory seems to tie in with the fact that heavy gambling is often associated with depression – though whether as cause or result is not fully known – and has been known to lead to suicide attempts.

For some experts on gambling, it's seen as a personality disorder, to be modified by psychotherapy of some kind; or a behavioural problem, which can respond to counselling or the help of Gamblers Anonymous. It's even thought that the addicted gambler may have a different chemistry from the rest of us.

Low self-esteem

Just as with drink or drug abuse, the reasons for getting addicted can vary from one individual to another but there is one core psychological factor which seems to apply to addicts of all kinds and that's lack of self-esteem.

This is evident in the gambler's obsessive need for affection and acceptance – a need that seems to me to be present in all of us all our lives, but the difference is in the word 'obsessive'. The gambler is *desperate* to be thought well of. He badly wants to be a winner at life as well as at the tables or racecourse. Yet, deep down, as long as he gambles, he's a loser, always a loser. There are no poor bookies or gambling operators – all a gambler has to do to lose is to go on gambling.

All the evidence is that addicts have had this low self-image long before they have become addicts. It is not the result of being humiliatingly in the grip of a compulsion, but the reason for it. Low self-esteem also makes someone very vulnerable to a take-over by an obsession, especially if it's one that will draw him out of his discontent with himself and his life into the seductive fantasies of being rich and powerful (in Gamblers Anonymous language, the 'dream world' of every problem gambler). Low self-esteem features very strongly in the profile of the average young gambler as well (see Chapter 8), which suggests it's there earlier rather than later in the problem gambler's history.

This, however, is an unconscious reason for gambling – no one, when asked, says 'I gamble because I don't think much of myself and winning will prove I'm somebody.' Anyone with a gambler in the family will probably be familiar with the reasons he gives for continuing to gamble. They are ways of justifying his gambling and reducing his guilt feelings, and they consist entirely of fantasies, the main one being that gambling will solve all his problems and make him a 'big man'. Some of these fantasies have been collected by the wife of a problem gambler.

- We owe two months' mortgage repayments – I haven't enough in the bank to cover it but I can easily win enough to clear it tomorrow.
- My wife deserves some fun – I'll spend my next big win on a holiday for her and her best friend in Bermuda. (He doesn't want to go himself – it would take him away from his gambling haunts.)
- My neighbours have no time for me. I'll show them I'm worth something. I'll get a silver Rolls and drive up and down the street.
- The debt-collectors have called again. I'll spend all day at the racecourse tomorrow and win enough to get them off my back.
- The least I can do for my children is to get them bikes as good as their friends have. I'll win even bigger and better bikes for them – they'll see what a great father I am . . .
- They're always putting me down at work. When I'm rich, I'll tell them where they can put their rotten job.
- My father still treats me like a little boy. One day soon, he'll find I'm someone to be reckoned with – he'll have to respect me for a change.

It's easy to see from the 'look-how-great-I-am' nature of this list that a male problem gambler is putting his masculinity on the line all the time – the opposite of the case with a female addict who doesn't consider her femininity to be at all involved in her gambling.

In fact, several studies have shown that gambling addicts strive for a machismo image and are fond of other risk-taking, masculine-type activities. In one study, by contrast, people who were not at all drawn to gambling expressed interest in a fixed salary, regular hours of work, music, art and sewing – a far cry from the joy in uncertainty and the breast-beating of the average male gambling addict.

Is there a problem gambler in your family?

It may be hard to tell. The difficulty with detecting a compulsive gambler is that, unlike other addictions, such as drugs or alcohol abuse, gambling has no obvious signs – no empty bottles or used needles lying around, no strong smells or tell-tale puncture marks. So you can remain blissfully ignorant for a long time if the gambler in your family wants to keep you in the dark. Another drawback is that addicts are absolute champions at lying and keeping secrets. It's interesting that we seem to have this facility when we're young but apparently grow out of it. Children are masters of the art of the blank, steady look when accused of anything, the injured innocence – 'Who? Me?' – followed by the unblushing denial. How can we not believe them? How cruel of us to suspect them!

Compulsive gamblers seem to be able to hang on to this facility in adulthood – perhaps it's a mark of their basic immaturity – and it takes a special brand of understanding in a partner to detect the changes in a gambler that spell trouble. In fact, his very secretiveness and evasion should alert you to the possibility that something is wrong.

Early warnings of a gambling addiction

- Unexplained absences from home.
- Continual lying about movements.
- Constant shortage of money.
- Increasing secretiveness generally.
- Neglect of work or studies, family, health and appearance.
- Agitation when unable to gamble (withdrawal symptoms).
- Mood swings.
- Loss of friends and social life.

At this stage, you could, with a superhuman effort, get the gambler to face up to the fact that he's on the brink of addiction. It's no use underestimating how difficult this might be. People who are addicted to gambling – or to anything else – always reckon that they can stop any time they want to, so they fiercely deny that their habit is getting out of control and that they need help.

Nevertheless, getting the heavy gambler to face up to his problems is the only help family and friends can give at this stage. He has to acknowledge that his gambling is out of control before he can accept the need for help. He may even deny that he gambles at all, whether you have proof or not, and you may even come to believe that the warning signs you've noted have some other explanation.

The most usual explanation that wives jump at is 'another woman'. Interestingly, some quizzing along these lines is usually enough to get the anxious gambler to come clean – 'No, honestly, I promise you, there's no one else, nobody. Proof? How can I prove it? There's no way. I haven't got another woman and that's that. No, you're wrong. Don't cry, you know I love you. I don't want anyone else. No, please. Oh, for goodness' sake, if you must know I was at the casino . . .'

Another way of getting at the truth is to be one step ahead of the gambler. For example, when he comes home from what you suspect was a trip to the betting-shop, you don't ask, 'Have you been gambling?' You ask, 'Did you win or lose?' It is that much more difficult to deny that he's been gambling when he first has to deal with your question – 'What do you mean – win or lose? Do you think I've been gambling? I don't know what you're talking about . . .' and so on.

Signs of a definite problem

- Huge debts – always explained away.
- Loss of job, or trouble at school or college about non-attendance.
- Unexplained 'borrowing' from family and friends.
- Evidence of stealing.
- A growing preoccupation with gambling until it's the only interest in his life.
- Complete alienation from friends and family – the gambler will have begged or stolen money from them at some time and been rejected ever since.
- Increasing tendency to gamble alone.

Profile of an addict

It would undoubtedly be useful if, faced with a gambler or two in the family or among our friends, we were able to tell who's likely to be a problem. Is it possible to tell who's going to be an addict and who isn't?

Well, not exactly. There's no hard evidence on what turns a social activity into a compulsion or why, but it's possible to compile the psychological profile of a potential addict from the many studies that have been made of compulsive gamblers:

- he's unwilling to accept reality
- he gambles to escape deeper problems
- he's insecure
- he wants good things without effort
- he has an urge to be a big shot
- he likes to compete – betting is a kind of battle but he doesn't accept that he is always ultimately the loser
- he feels guilty (not necessarily about gambling) and his losses are a way of punishing himself
- he may be depressed
- he lacks self-esteem and self-confidence.

The list above could fit any compulsive gambler who frequents racecourses, betting-shops and casinos. There is another profile compiled by a psychiatrist which is more applicable to the high-profile kind of gambler who plays the financial markets and up-market casinos, winning and losing in millions rather than hundreds and thousands. It could equally well apply to the new generation of managers and market-men and the international tycoons who are forever buying and selling corporations and launching new companies – but then they are risk-takers and gamblers too, at heart, and may have the following characteristics:

- contempt for moderate earnings
- constant inner tension
- highly ambitious, tends to overwork
- dissatisfaction and boredom if deprived of new opportunities to show off or succeed
- competitive and a bad loser
- cynical and hypersensitive
- contempt for unsuccessful people
- I-know-better-attitude
- health worries without cause
- inability to enjoy simple pleasures of life
- hidden depression shown by exaggerated air of importance.

You might recognize a family member in this profile. His form of gambling will probably be the risks and buzz of the business world; his career is the main stake; power, prestige and big money are the prizes. Other things he puts on the line are friends, family and the feeling side of life.

A recent study of compulsive gamblers in the US found that family background was very important in the development of their compulsion. Common factors were:

- from a broken, disruptive or very poor family
- heavy emphasis on money in the family
- the death of a parent or parental figure in gambler's childhood
- serious injury or illness in the family, or to the gambler himself
- infidelity by parents or gambler's partner
- high incidence of verbal, physical and sexual abuse involving gambler
- gambler has felt rejected as a child and often humiliated as an adult
- underlying features of all the compulsive gamblers in this study was not knowing how to turn to others for help and using gambling as a form of escape.

When Irene, a 43-year-old divorcee, saw this list, she was amazed how well it fitted her ex-husband, a problem gambler since he was 16.

I always knew he'd had a rotten childhood but I never thought it had anything to do with the gambling. His mother was cold as ice. Fortunately, I didn't have much to do with her – she kept her distance. I don't think she had any feelings for Chris at all, never had by the sound of it.

I gather that the start of it was that Chris had had a twin brother until they were about five. They weren't identical – his brother Michael was much better looking. I've seen a photo of the two of them – the only one Chris has, and Chris, who's a nice-looking bloke now, tall and slim, looks like an odd-shaped lump of nothing beside this godlike little boy with golden hair and a proud sort of look – talk about little Lord Fauntleroy, he even had a sailor suit while Chris was in a boring sort of smock and shorts.

Of course, their mother adored Michael and, from what I can gather, pretty well ignored Chris, except for comparing him with Michael most of the time and pushing him about and slapping him. He can't remember any cuddles or bedtime stories or anything – I could cry about it now. His father was no help because he always sided with his mother – Chris thinks he absolutely adored her and never denied her anything, so it sounds as if he treated Chris like something the cat brought in as well.

Then it all becomes too awful and confused for Chris to remember. He loved his brother. In spite of the difference, they were apparently quite close – there's something about twins, isn't there? They're never really separate, I've heard, always some part of them is with the other one.

Anyway, one day Michael was ill in bed at home having a terrific fuss made of him and the next day he was away in hospital, Chris thinks, and he never saw him again. Nobody told him anything. As if it wasn't bad enough that he'd lost his twin brother, his mother apparently decided from that day on that Chris wasn't her son – she couldn't bear to look at him, he remembers, and she sent him to his granny in Suffolk. She was a dear but she couldn't make up for parents who didn't want him or for his lost brother.

When we married I could see that he thought nothing of himself and I thought I could help him. Underneath, he was so kind and gentle but so lost. On top, he became rather a pain – always suspicious of being bested or put down. I knew he gambled but didn't know he needed it so badly. He was clever, brilliant at figures and made quite a lot of money as an accountant so he could quite easily go mad at the bookies before we began to feel the pinch. He just went on until we were on our beam-ends, denying all the time that he was addicted or that there was any problem. I had to get a divorce just to get a life. I can see now that he couldn't help any of it. His childhood had been really horrific. He needed counselling, I suppose. That would have been a good answer. A mother who cared for him would have been an even better one . . .

The change from regular gambler to problem gambler can be very gradual. What essentially distinguishes the casual or regular from the problem gambler is the element of compulsion – how badly he wants to make bets. At first, the compulsion may be quite weak. You may notice that your partner or whoever gambles in your family is simply increasing the time he spends on gambling without any obvious compulsion about it. Then he gets to the stage where he doesn't want to spend his leisure time in any other way.

The next step is that he's driven to cut out other elements of his life which he feels interfere with his gambling. The first things to go are family occasions and outings. Then socializing with friends is given a miss, next he's skiving off work and having to give excuses to his employers and lie to his wife. This is when deception starts in a big way, and so does the borrowing, the debts and the stealing. By now the magnetic pull towards the next bet governs the gambler's whole life. He has become an addict.

Some of the things that addicts will do when they're really hooked are hard to believe, even by the gamblers themselves when they look back. Dennis, who ran his own hairdressing business a few doors away from a betting-shop, was spending more time in the bookies than at work.

I began taking money out of the till – just grabbing handfuls of notes and going along to the bookies. I figured it was my money anyway – it was *my* business and *my* customers' money they'd paid to *me* – so why shouldn't I do what I liked with it? At the time, I couldn't see that this was what paid all the overheads of the place, the staff's wages, etc. I wasn't concerned. I needed the money to bet with, so I used it.

It took several months for the place to go completely bust. I had to sack all the staff, no compensation or anything – I told them it was all due to them, they hadn't managed to keep our customers or get in more. I thought it was a smart move, letting the business go down the tubes. It saved me all the overheads and all the worry – it went into liquidation owing thousands, mostly income tax and VAT, and I thought, 'Now I'm free to gamble as much as I like.' But, of course, there was no till to draw from and my wife took over our joint account so I was completely zapped. One thing I couldn't do was steal, though I borrowed as much as I could until that dried up. Finally, I gave in, got very depressed, saw the doc and ended up with GA.

Several Gamblers Anonymous members have described how they'd broken into their children's money boxes, pawned a partner's jewellery, stolen a father's golfing trophies. One was at the dog-track the night before his wedding and lost all the money he'd saved for the honeymoon. Another refused to visit his wife in hospital in the evenings, which was when she begged him to come and cheer her up, because he had to be at the casino until the small hours. He was gambling when she was discharged and she had to walk home from the hospital. While another man's wife and children were on holiday, he gambled away the rent money and sold all the family's insurance policies.

They all had tales of how low they had descended to raise funds for gambling – Gavin appeared to have sunk lower than most.

I tell you what, there was nothing I wouldn't do. I only needed half a crown in the old money to start me off. I'd return lemonade bottles and get 2d off each – I'd liberate them from dumps and dustbins if there weren't enough at home. Nearly every day I dug deep down the sides of the sofa for the odd coin – the adrenalin used to start running while I was just looking for money.

I spent my nineteenth birthday in court for stealing from a charity flag-seller in the street. Later on, I had loans from several banks for cars and spent it all on gambling and then I moved in on banks and building societies. Stick-ups weren't so dicey then – they didn't have TV and cameras all over the place. But after my last stretch in prison my wife said she'd had enough – she'd been strong up to then – I thought, 'This is a useless lark' and she nagged me to get help.

I haven't had a bet for three years – although I'm still a compulsive gambler at heart, you understand. It's only now that I realize how the gambling urge can degrade you. It puts you right down in the pits. You have to realize how low you are before you can drag yourself up. It needs humility – and that's hard, I can tell you, for a man who's always reckoned his next bet's going to make him the lord of creation.

Most addicted gamblers' stories are remarkably similar. They all seem to follow the same well-worn path with no stops on the way. The path has the following steps:

- marital problems
- debts
- creditors putting pressure on
- loss of job
- isolation
- legal problems
- criminal activities.

The trouble is that the problem gambler sees no reason to stop on this race to ruin. He's so heavily defended by denial against any recognition of his problems that things have to get very bad indeed before he will throw in the towel. The usual trigger is loss or threatened loss of something very important to the gambler, i.e. his wife, children or home. The most common scenario is that if he loses one of these, he loses all three.

So most gambling addicts literally have to reach despair – their personal rock-bottom, as GA puts it – before admitting the need for help. That's why it's very difficult for a wife or friend to intervene successfully at any step of the downward path. Nevertheless, it can be done and I show you how in Chapter 5. There is also the support and help of Gam-Anon, GA's 'sister' organization for the families of compulsive gamblers – more about this in Chapter 6.

4

The gambler's family

The gambler's effect on his or her family can be devastating – more devastating, perhaps, than with any other compulsive behaviour, even including infidelity. With compulsive gambling the crisis comes after a long, slow downhill slide and, when it comes, it's more likely to have long-term effects on the family, both practically and psychologically. Infidelity may be a crushing emotional blow to the adulterer's partner but it doesn't normally bankrupt the adulterer and rob him of his wife, children, home, job and standing in the community. That's what gambling can do.

Family life

Marie is the daughter of a gambling addict. She's a successful business woman in her forties and has never married.

We had a home in the suburbs and father went by train to the City every day. Apparently, horse-racing was his particular addiction and he had accounts with several bookmakers near where he worked. I remember him poring over the *Sporting Life* and I was aware of many times when the telephone and gas were cut off and the radio was in hock.

It was a very gradual thing, spread over the time when I was about five to when I was 18, but what he did in the end was gamble away everything he had. We were always on the move from one small home to a smaller one and they were all pitifully equipped with stuff from sales and Woolworths. I remember once coming home from school to find the bailiffs had been in to recover yet another debt and where there'd been a settee and armchairs to sit on, there were now two deckchairs and some packing-cases.

The effect on the family was to drag us all down to rock-bottom but he couldn't see that he had a problem. Even when he was ill in hospital and, as it turned out, on his deathbed, he still persuaded one of the nurses to put bets on for him – a gambling man to his last breath.

For me, it all sowed the seeds of a lifelong sense of insecurity. I've become fiercely independent and can't trust anyone to care for me financially or emotionally – certainly not any man. I constantly fear being let down. As a result, I find it hard to get close to people and I'm rather lonely. It's a funny thing, though – I do get a lottery ticket every week. I tell myself it's because it gives me something to look forward to when the results come up. But perhaps there's some gambling blood in my veins.

This story is not unusual. Hundreds of gamblers' lives have followed a similar pattern and their families suffered similar effects. There are probably an equal number of gamblers' children, however, who've been affected in the opposite way and, far from seeing a wager as a bit of light entertainment, have themselves become heavy gamblers.

Bill was a gambler for 28 years, lost one wife, home and family and reduced a second family to poverty. He says he started gambling because his dad gambled.

He used to bet on dogs and horses with the street bookies. Sometimes he'd go to the course and take me with him. It was tremendously exciting, especially when he won. I suppose you could say that I was being conditioned to the thrill you can get from gambling.

We lived at the seaside where there were lots of arcades and I started playing the machines. Then I moved on to horses and dogs. My parents weren't at all worried – my dad was in control of his gambling so they couldn't see any harm in it. At 17, I won a big one – it was thousands. I kept it secret from my parents and used it to start me off on a gambling career – I think I was well and truly hooked by that time. I lost so much through it, including all my self-respect. I'm still recovering, after seven years without a bet. I wish to hell I'd never started. I want to forgive my father but I can't.

A lot of compulsive gambling is due to parents' misguided support of their adult child's habit. They often become overprotective, with a martyr-like attitude to the demands the gambler puts on them. 'Oh, isn't it awful? We'll have to get him out of trouble again . . .' they say, relishing the fact that he's still dependent on them. They continually bail him out and won't allow him to take responsibility for himself. As a result, he remains immature, irresponsible and guilt-free whilst success-fully manipulating his parents to carry these loads for him.

The wife

The gambler, well into both addiction and denial of it by this time, will go on to behave in exactly the same way to his wife – blaming her for his compulsion and expecting her to carry the responsibility for all its consequences. It's time to ask why women take up with gamblers in the first place, and why do they stay with them?

One reason which has to be mentioned, although the evidence for it is only anecdotal, is that gamblers tend to be charming people. Living on a knife-edge as they often do, they are aware of other people's feelings and needs and can be very responsive to them – except when their own needs are felt to be greater. Their promises to stop gambling and their fantasies about why they gamble are extremely convincing. Compulsive gamblers are also very appealing in their favourite role of 'little boy lost' – a role which works wonders with women of all sorts, even those with sharp brains and stony hearts.

The trouble is that gamblers, having deceived and charmed their partners successfully year after year, start to believe their own lies and eventually cannot distinguish reality from truth. This is known to recovering addicts as the gambler's 'dream world' and it is very hard to get out of.

However, if you're now the wife of a problem gambler you're not likely, on your wedding day, to have had an inkling of what lies in store when you are married. A study of compulsive gamblers and their families in the US has shown that of the 90 per cent of wives who didn't know about their husband's gambling problem when they married, a third found out soon after the wedding and two-thirds only became aware of the problem several years after the marriage; 10 per cent of the problem gamblers' wives did know about the problem but thought marriage and family would cure their husbands.

The wives in this survey were not ignorant of the fact that their husbands were serious or regular gamblers – only unaware that the gambling was a *problem*, i.e. that their partners were either addicted or getting that way. This is true of all partnerships involving gambling – the non-gambling partner is attracted unconsciously to the very qualities that have made the other partner a gambler and moreover, one at risk of addiction. In short, although she may later see herself as purely the *victim* of a gambling addict, she herself contributes something, however small, to his gambling habit and is herself getting something out of it.

What does she get out of it? We saw in Chapter 3 how the main trigger for the gambling habit is the gambler's low self-esteem. I also referred earlier in this chapter to the way that a compulsive gambler counts on his parents to protect him from the consequences of his gambling. These two factors have a strong appeal to a potential partner who both has doubts about her own value and also is happy to take on the parental role that her husband will readily transfer to her from his real parents – especially the role of mother.

This is why, in many cases of addiction, both partners have to change before there can really be a 'cure'. I go into this further in the next chapter. The new wife is, of course, untroubled by all these psychological undercurrents and embarks blissfully on the steps that will eventually force them both to meet the problem head-on.

Step One – At first, the wife may enjoy going with her husband and their friends to the casino or racetrack. It's social activity and it's fun. He makes light of his losses so she trusts him to know what he's doing.

Step Two – She notices how preoccupied and tense he is while gambling, so much so that he virtually ignores her. His gambling friends' wives don't accompany them any more. It all begins to pall and she stops going. He fails to hide his relief.

Step Three – He stays out a lot more with some feeble explanations and is often on a short fuse when he comes back. She begins to get very worried but is soothed by his reassurances that he'll soon be a winner and all will be well. She also begins to adapt to his addiction with strategies, described later in this chapter, which actually make the problem worse.

Step Four – He goes over the top and is quite obviously compelled to gamble whatever the cost. They argue and fight – the relationship self-destructs and nothing is left but the need for help.

All this happens so gradually and with so many jerks between hope that the gambling is not as bad as it seems and despair at proof that it is, that sometimes it can be hard to tell exactly what you're up against. To help you clear the picture, ask yourself the following questions:

- Are debt collectors starting to call?
- Is he out for long periods without explanation?
- Is he untrustworthy with money, e.g. spends earmarked sums on something else?

- Does he keep borrowing money?
- Does he keep promising to stop gambling – but always breaks his promise?
- Has he changed in many ways from the person you married?
- Do you have to hide money from him?
- Does he try to hide money from you?
- Does he avoid talking about gambling?
- Does he blame you for the fact that he wants to gamble?
- Do you feel forced into controlling his life?
- Are you anxious about him getting into serious trouble?

If your answer is 'yes' to more than half of these questions, your partner is forcing you to be the kind of person you wouldn't want to know – anxious, angry, suspicious, bossy and controlling. You're also gradually being driven into either playing his games – 'Yes, I'll be mother', or into playing some games of your own – 'I'll make you feel as unloved as you make me feel.' Bear in mind that a wife in this situation is not just her husband's partner. She's a person in her own right with needs of her own too. What are they?

- To be loved.
- To be needed.
- To be in control – both of the problem situation and also of the person who's causing it.

As well as these three overriding emotional needs, she will also have a major practical one – to survive this crisis and, if there are children, to bring them safely through it too.

Her need to be loved gets short shrift. It meets with rejection at every turn. Her husband's back is always towards her, all his thoughts and longings facing the next chance to gamble. She begins to feel that her husband can't love her if he can ignore and hurt her so cruelly. She can scarcely be expected to understand that he simply isn't controlling his actions. He doesn't gamble to hurt her, he gambles because he must – it is his sickness that is hurting her. Also, in the same way that drugs dull the senses, a gambling addiction can kill all the normal responses to people you love. Feelings of affection and concern may be there, but they cannot be shown – they are too deeply buried under the overwhelming urge to gamble.

The result is often the feeling that 'If he doesn't love me anymore, it must be my fault. I don't deserve to be loved . . .' ending up with a crippling lack of self-esteem. What follows is what always follows a dive in self-confidence or self-esteem – a desperate struggle to get back on top and in charge. Success in this struggle will mean that she will feel both needed and also in control.

In the bid to be needed, the wife is likely to do some or all of the following:

- lie for her husband to his employer
- lie for him to anyone to whom he owes money
- ask her family or in-laws for money
- excuse his behaviour to herself and others
- when possible, act as guarantor for loans for him
- do anything she can to keep him out of trouble, including prison
- pay up for bounced cheques he's written.

In the bid to be in control, her tactics will mostly be ones that put her husband down and show how useless he is as a man and as a husband. She is not to blame for this – she is now as driven as he is. His escape is into gambling. At first, she has no escape.

- she lets the children see how little she respects him and argues with him in front of them
- she treats him like one of the children and lays down the law
- she searches his clothes, car, papers for signs of debt or anything to do with gambling
- she tries to trap him into admissions of lying about where he's been and what he was doing
- she controls their sex-lives – either by refusing sex or 'giving way' to it
- she emphasizes how little she cares about him by not bothering about the state of the home, the meals, his clothes and her appearance
- she has fantasies of having an affair to pay him out
- she goes for an obsession of her own to get even – drink, religion, nights out with 'the girls'.

The trouble with all these ploys is that, by making him feel useless and no good, they are driving him with greater force towards the bookies or the croupier. The lower he feels, the more he needs the 'high' of gambling.

All these self-defeating games – the 'mothering', the complete take-over of responsibility, the put-downs and angry acting out – do not result in a cure or even in getting the compulsive gambler to a source of help. In the next chapter we'll see what tactics are likely to solve the problem and how a wife can cope meanwhile.

The children

Although a problem gambler's children are not usually blamed for his addiction, as his wife invariably is, in all other respects and in different ways they are just as deeply affected by a compulsive gambler in the family – usually even more so because they have absolutely no control over what is happening to the only world they know. Even quite young children, from about three or four years old, can become the victims of gambling because of what they gather from the emotional atmosphere in the family and how they interpret it.

Even more telling are the consequences for the child of the way the adults handle the changes and crises caused by having a compulsive gambler in the family. It's very similar to the effect of divorce on the children. It is not the fact of divorce which decides whether they are going to be problem children or come through the experience in good heart, but the way the divorce is managed – how sensitively their fears are handled, how honest the parents are, how fully and appropriately for their age they're told about what's happening and so on.

So it is with the child victim of a compulsive gambling parent – the handling can damage him for life or it can leave him feeling sad for a while, perhaps, but at least free of guilt, resentment and self-hate.

A workshop held recently by some gamblers and Gam-Anon members in the UK produced six typical scenarios and, from personal experience, showed what effect they are likely to have on a child or children directly involved.

1 Parent being arrested and the child being bundled off to a relative and not told what was happening.
Effect Child may feel rejected and not trusted, imagining all kinds of terrible reasons for father's disappearance including the possibility that he, the child, is to blame. He may also grieve for his absent father.

2 Child being told elaborate lies to cover up the fact that parent is in prison.
Effect Child will be confused, know there is something very wrong and feel let down. If he learns the truth later, it will be a severe shock leading to feelings of sadness, anger and guilt.

3 The mother, in the absence of her partner, will turn to the child for emotional support.
Effect Again, the child will be confused about his role and forced to take on inappropriate responsibilities, thus missing out on childhood.

4 Child is expected by either parent to keep secrets from the other parent, tell lies and back up the ongoing pattern of deceit between the parents.
Effect The child will have to cope with split loyalties and be forced to keep secrets and lies when it feels all wrong – and be given a bad example of dishonesty and deceit for later life.

5 In order to regain the attention and affection of the parents a child often starts to model himself or herself on the same-sex parent.
Effect A son becomes a gambler. A daughter becomes a 'victim'.

6 Debts, arguments, visits by creditors, threatening phone calls will cause tension and anxiety in the home.
Effect This atmosphere cannot be hidden. As when divorce or separation is in the air, children will pick up on all the unhappiness and may feel responsible for it. In both cases, telling the child the truth will spare them some painful and unnecessary fantasies.

It's useful to look at what's happening in a compulsive gambler's family from the child's point of view. Luckily, we have some help here. Wanda, a member of a Gam-Anon group, has listed some of the things the son or daughter of a problem gambler will observe in everyday life at home:

• constant conflict between the parents
• father's withdrawal from the family
• collapse of father's role as head of the family
• mother's unpredictable behaviour to all the family
• mother's anger displaced on to children
• father's denials of anything wrong and his phoney optimism
• breakdown of communication between the parents and between child and father
• the child starts to see the father as a complete phoney who might abandon the family, and take all their money and possessions with him.

In short, children in this situation become insecure, confused and very anxious. They cannot simply accept these painful feelings. How do they respond? Again, Wanda from Gam-Anon tells us, starting with a son's likely reactions.

- he tries, and fails, to recover his father's interest and affection
- he represses his feelings
- he avoids confrontation
- he copes with stress like his father does, i.e. walks away from disagreements, won't talk about his problems, behaves in ways that make him feel big
- he sides with Dad against his 'bossy' mother and, like Dad, starts to manipulate her
- he feels torn because he's dependent on his father for security
- he feels under pressure of these conflicting emotions, withdraws from family
- he feels responsible for family's problems, hopeless about making things better, and develops low self-esteem.

Daughters react to a gambling father with much the same pain and confusion but the breakdown of the relationship with him differs from a son's in two vital ways.

- It's likely to affect all her future relationships with the opposite sex, making it hard for her to respect men and easy to view them as weak and irresponsible.
- Her self-esteem, dependent to a great extent on the approval and encouragement of a strong, loving father, will never really get off the ground.

As we have seen, low self-esteem is one of the prime triggers for compulsive gambling so, for both boys and girls, there is already a link between gambler-parent and potentially gambling child. This is why therapy for the whole family is often considered the best treatment for compulsive gamblers. It not only aims to change the gambler but also hopes to prevent the chain of relationship breakdown and escape-into-addiction extending into the next generation and beyond.

However, the influence on the child is not always towards gambling. Sometimes it's towards another lifestyle that might produce problems of a different kind or, at best, a life that's less than fulfilled.

Derek's story is an example. Now 50, he clearly remembers his early childhood when his father, a hotel manager, started to become addicted to card games.

We lived in the hotel and I was their only child. My father used to set up card-games with local friends and with people staying in the hotel – I think they mostly played poker.

The atmosphere in the hotel, especially on card-playing nights, was very masculine – full of cigar smoke and whisky smells and guffaws of laughter, and I can remember my father strutting about in a very boastful, macho way when he'd won.

In the 1950s, he switched to playing in a casino. He began stealing the hotel takings to finance the game and eventually we had to move out. He ran a café instead and we lived on top – it was appalling. I vowed I'd get my mother away from him and the awful life she was leading. When I was 25 I was running a very successful antiques business and I took my mother to live with me. She divorced my father. My mother always says he was just weak but I think he was utterly selfish and never cared for her or for me.

We're both strongly against gambling in all its forms. I can't even understand why anyone should ever want to buy a lottery ticket – not with those odds. They must all be mad.

There is, of course, nothing that the children of a gambler can do to change their father or alter the consequences of his gambling. Up to their teens, it's their mother who has to cope with the fall-out and get help. However, through her, it's possible for them to come to terms with the family situation, whether it stays in one piece or breaks down.

When they're old enough, most, like Derek, will deal with their pain by getting well away from the problem parent. Others, especially those who feel duty-bound to care for their problem parent, will stay and try, in their turn, to 'mother' the compulsive gambler. This was Rosie's way of coping with her mother.

I think it was Dad's constant womanizing that drove her to bingo. All the family knew when he had a girlfriend. She'd hammer away at him until he admitted it – I can't understand why she didn't just let it alone. Perhaps it was because he was actually very good to her, especially when he had a girlfriend. He treated her as if she were an invalid – which I suppose she was really, an emotional invalid anyway. She just couldn't cope with life.

She started on bingo with an older friend who was always coming round with comforting noises for Mum. First they went just one afternoon a week to a tiny, converted old cinema up the road. Then it was a big place, more professional, with a caller and a mike and, finally, where she goes now which is the only bingo place for miles and has everything mechanized. While it was still in the little place nearby, Mum became really hooked. She went every time it was open. She spent the food money, the rent money, my school dinner money, any money she could lay her hands on. If she won – which she did sometimes – she'd squirrel it away for more bingo later. She has to go on a bit of a bus-ride now. When she wins she blows it all on taxis.

My father used to turn a blind eye, just give her much less money for housekeeping and take care of the rent and other bills himself. But it got so that she wasn't lifting a finger in the house – by the time I was 12, I was doing it all. My brother went off to college after leaving school and he doesn't bother coming home much. My father's living with another woman the other side of town. He still gives Mum some money and of course I'm earning now.

It's an addiction all right. You should see how animated she is when she's about to take off for bingo. I couldn't leave her. She'll have to come and live with us if I ever get married. I honestly think she'd be dead if it weren't for bingo. I'm here to keep her going to bingo and staying alive. One good thing is that I'll never ever go to a bingo game.

What a gambling parent did for Rosie was to make her swap roles. Her Mum was the helpless, vulnerable child and Rose was the mother. She perhaps could have, in time, persuaded her mother to get GA's help. But that was evidently not Rosie's choice – and no one can say it was a wrong or right choice. In Chapter 5, I describe further choices for the families of gambling addicts.

5

Coping with problem gambling

When we were looking at the effect of compulsive gambling on the gambler's family (Chapter 4), we saw that, by putting all his immaturity and lack of responsibility on to his partner, he begins to see her as 'mother' rather than 'wife' and his own role as a dependant rather than an equal. Like the schoolboy who looks to his mother to get him out of scrapes, he relies on his wife to come to the rescue when his addiction gets him into difficulties.

This is one reason why it's pointless for me or you or anyone else to offer advice to the gambler himself on how to get over his addiction. He wouldn't listen. He doesn't admit he has a problem. He doesn't need your advice or your help, thank you. All he wants is for the world to keep the money supply coming, bail him out when he's in trouble and leave him alone to get on with his gambling. 'The world', in this context, is whoever he's using to do his worrying, borrowing and cover-ups for him – in most cases, his wife.

Now his wife could actually welcome this dependence on her because she might, like many women, have an outsize need to be needed. Psychologists reckon that this is what often draws women unconsciously into partnerships with addicts or potential addicts – she meets his need for a prop and he meets her need to be one.

This was borne out by the large number of letters in my problem post from women who had finally freed themselves from husbands who were alcoholics or compulsive gamblers, gone straight into a second marriage, and found – surprise and horrors – that the second husband has a drink or gambling problem too and is leaning on her for all he's worth.

A woman who welcomes a partner's dependence on her will foster it rather than help him to tackle the reason for it. If she doesn't welcome his dependence, or she realizes that leaning on her is not helping him to break his addiction, what can she do? The alternatives are:

- accept she's in a bind and stay with him as 'mother'
- risk changing to 'wife' and help him grow up
- end the relationship.

Let's suppose that you're facing these choices. If you stay with him as 'mother', his addiction will continue until you're forced into the third option.

45

The risk of changing to 'wife' is that he'll go off and find another 'mother' – but it isn't inevitable. You could stop being 'mother' to your gambling husband but still keep the relationship going. How can you do that?

Ways to stop mothering

Consistently refuse to accept responsibility for his gambling

He tries to put the blame on you – 'You drive me to it with your nagging', 'If you spent less on the kids and yourself I wouldn't be in debt', 'It's your fault your parents won't help us out – you don't do anything to keep them sweet.' He's talking as if you had some influence over his gambling. You haven't. No one has. Resist the idea that it's in your power to stop him gambling. It isn't. His is the problem. His is the responsibility. His alone is the power to break out of his addiction. All you can do is get him to the point where he realizes he has a problem and makes his own decision to get help.

Don't play his games

He picks fights so that it gives him an excuse to slam out of the house and make for the betting-shop, race-track or casino. Don't fight. Don't join the game. Point out straightaway what he's doing and why.

Don't pretend to believe his lies

It's often easier to turn a blind eye to an obvious attempt to deceive you about where he's been or how much money he's lost – much harder to show, without going off the handle, that you're aware he's lying. He'll deny he's taken the rent, forged a cheque, lost the holiday money or whatever and be really aggrieved if you don't believe him. 'Why won't you ever trust me?', 'I give you my word – isn't that good enough?' etc.

Nevertheless, you have to show you know the truth. Then make it clear that you condemn the lies but not the liar. He'll eventually respect you more for not allowing him to deceive you. Remember how wet we thought our parents were when we successfully pulled the wool over their eyes?

Don't join in his fantasies

He tells you he gambles to make life better for you, to give you everything you want, to give the kids 'more than I had', to pay back all his debts in one fell swoop, to get a bigger house, to show his father how

46

smart he is, to take the family on the holiday of a lifetime – there's no end to the justification he can dream up for his desire to go on gambling.

What you have to do is keep on bringing him back to earth and to reality. 'Yes, that would be nice, but first let's buy a TV licence.' 'How about paying the gas bill before you think of taking us to Disneyland?' 'The car we've got goes all right – I'm happy with it. Why waste money on a new one?'

There's no need to nag about it – just matter-of-factly bring him out of his dream-land and into reality. He has to face the bitter truth – that he is never, ever, going to win that kind of money – no compulsive gambler does. The only people to make anything out of gambling are the bookies, the professional gamblers and the casino owners. The gamblers who lose the most are the ones who can't stop, win or lose.

Stop rescuing him from crises

Don't lie for him, borrow for him, guarantee loans, repay bounced cheques, make excuses for him, or neglect the rest of the family to help him. If you do this much for him, he'll never be able to face crises without your help.

Ask friends and family not to help him – even if it means he ends up in prison. As Gamblers Anonymous says, 'Every gambler has to reach his own rock-bottom before climbing up again.' This means that your efforts to get him to face up to the problem might have no success at all until he has absolutely no way to turn in order to avoid disaster. Even when disaster looms, don't be tempted to do a rescue act. All this will do is painfully postpone the moment of reckoning and the start of the endgame when he's ready to help himself.

Don't act how you feel – tell him

As the weeks go by and more and more promises are broken, you're bound to become distrustful, then angry, then downright hostile. If you act out this hostility by, for example, refusing sex or meals, it gives him the opportunity to say, 'You see, that's why I gamble! Look at the way you treat me' – and he will gamble even more.

If, on the other hand, you simply say how you feel, calmly and firmly – 'I'm getting to the end of my tether. I can see us losing everything, including each other. Won't you please do something about your gambling before I have to walk out?' Put it like this and he can't put the blame for his gambling on to you – you have put it firmly on his shoulders and told him what could happen if he doesn't get help.

Don't ever make a threat without meaning it and, if it comes to that, carrying it through. In many cases, a compulsive gambler hasn't considered for a moment the idea that his marriage could break up until his wife actually moves herself and the children away for a few months. The compulsive gambler might continue on his own until the real crunch comes – prison or suicide (unhappily, they are always a possibility). Or this break in the pattern of his life could jolt him finally into looking into the future and seeing that he doesn't have any, not without his family or his self-respect.

When Linda first suspected that her husband's gambling was out of control she admits now that she did all the wrong things.

Without realizing it, I was doing everything to keep Joe's gambling going – drawing money out for him, juggling our debts, going on the beg to my grandparents. I was ashamed that he gambled at all, let alone that it was getting out of hand. I didn't want anyone to know so I lied for him and after a while it was hard to know who was telling the most lies, him or me.

To family and friends I pretended that we were having a hard time because my husband had an enormous income tax bill to pay – well, he had but he wasn't paying it. He was self-employed, running a garden maintenance business, but every time he actually did some work he'd ask to be paid in cash and, of course, it all went on the horses.

Luckily, or unluckily as it turned out, I had some money left from my share of the house that I and my first husband owned and I also had a job at the children's school during term-time. I was baling him out all the time from my savings until there just wasn't any left. I honestly don't know why I did it. Perhaps it was because I believed him when he said he had a sure-fire system which was going to pay off in a big way and then he'd pay me back hundredfold and start afresh. I wanted to believe him. I couldn't face the truth any more than he could.

After all the savings had gone, I was a bit more careful but I still drew money out of my current account whenever he said he was desperate. He had a marvellous way with him – talk about charm. I was putty in his hands.

It was my smashing granny who put me on the right track. I'd spent a lot of time with her as a child. We used to share everything and in the end I couldn't lie to her any more – she'd been a brick coming up with a few hundred now and then when I said we'd had some big bill or other and that Joe's business was suffering from the recession. She didn't buy any of this apparently – after I'd confessed what the trouble was, she told me she knew all along.

We talked it over. She said I had to let Joe find his own level – it was no use propping him up. So then I became a real monster – it was terribly hard because I've always loved him. I refused to give him any money and I made damn sure there wasn't any lying about, no cheque-books or credit cards either.

He still had some regular customers and I asked them to pay by cheque made out to the business. I told his brother, who sometimes lent him money, not to do it anymore – thank goodness he agreed to go along with this when he realized it was Joe's only hope. And I stopped asking the grandparents for hand-outs.

It was all down to Joe now and he was furious. He accused me of treachery and meanness, said I obviously didn't love him if I could treat him like this. The rows were awful – I don't know where his charm went. The only good thing about that dreadful time is that I didn't have the worry of complete destitution for me and the kids – everything we had was in my name and I had charge of all the outgoings. We just about kept our heads above water – but Joe was sinking fast.

I didn't know, until the police came for him, that he'd been going out housebreaking and robbing post offices. It was really serious stuff – he'd been going to the races, apparently, with his pockets stuffed with thousands of pounds in cash. If he ever won, I never saw a penny of it – he probably put it all back on the horses.

Once he was in prison, I was all for dropping the monster act and making him as comfortable as possible. I reckoned he'd learnt his lesson and it would all be OK when he came out. But Gran said, 'No. What makes you think he's learnt his lesson? Has he said anything yet about getting help? He's not going to help himself at all if he thinks you're still going to mother him.' So I kept it up – I visited but didn't take any comforts and all we talked about was how he was going to go to GA when he got out.

For a couple of weeks after he was free, it looked as if he was going to go back to his old ways – he was having terrible withdrawal symptoms and slunk off several times saying he was going to see his brother but it must have been the betting-shop because he came back even deeper in the dumps and couldn't look me in the eye. Every day I really hammered at him to go for help – I was ready to leave him if he wouldn't and he knew it. But I didn't want to lose him – I wanted the old Joe back that I married – the one who never wanted to give me a moment's unhappiness.

So I stayed tough – it was our only chance. One day I was so furious and frustrated that I locked him in the bathroom and wouldn't let him out until he said he'd go to GA. At last he said he would. I already knew when the next meeting of our nearest branch was – I'd had all the information about them for three years – so I walked him round there on the night and that was it. Later, when he'd been to several meetings, we had a celebration. He knew he wasn't out of the wood yet by a long chalk but he was so *pleased* with himself for taking that first step. We had a bottle of champagne and I did a super meal at home for us, the girls and my grandparents. I've never been so happy.

A gambler's wife who doesn't have a gran like Linda's can get the same kind of help by going along to a meeting of Gam-Anon for the family and friends of problem gamblers. This contact with other wives will show you that you're not alone in your struggles and will bring you the support that only fellow-sufferers can give each other. However, Gam-Anon does a lot more than that. You will find a full account in the next chapter.

How do a problem gambler's children cope?

In Chapter 4 on the gambler's family, we saw how a father's compulsive gambling can affect his children by making them anxious, insecure, confused, manipulative and very unhappy. I also made the point that, just as in the case of divorce, the extent to which the children are damaged by the upheaval in the family depends almost entirely on the way the crisis is handled and how they are helped to deal with their feelings about what's happening.

Unfortunately, again like divorce, problem gambling in the family is yet another situation which puts most of the burden on to one parent. In divorce, it's likely to be the parent with whom the children live who has to be responsible for responding to the children's real needs and avoiding lasting damage – and that's usually the mother. However, this isn't to say that the absent parent can't play an equal part, if he so minds, in the damage limitation.

The ideal outcome is when both father and mother are at pains to preserve a good image – neither saintly nor devilish – of the other parent in the child's mind and also maintain, as far as possible, the child's relationship with both parents. The dangers to avoid are feelings that he's been rejected by one or both parents, a fear that he's to blame for the split, and anxiety about his place in the world in view of all this chaos and uncertainty. So the essence of help for the child is to restore his sense of security, self-esteem and trust.

When there's a problem gambler in the family, it's not so clear-cut.

50

The gambler cannot respond to the childrens' anxieties and confusion in any way. If he notices it, he will say it's all down to his wife because she's always nagging him and trying to restrict his pleasure. The tension in the house, the children's divided loyalties are all her fault – she causes them by refusing to behave like a 'proper wife'.

The result is that, in handling the children's worries, mother is on her own. She's not going to get any help from her husband. He'll deny that the children are affected by his gambling as strongly as he denies the gambling itself. If you're in this situation, however, don't despair. You can lessen the risks to your children, even without your husband's help, in the following ways.

- *Explain very clearly what the problem is.* If a child doesn't know what's going on, he'll imagine something much more fearful than the reality. Fit what you say and how you say it to the understanding and age of the child.

- *Put things as simply as possible.* For example, to a six-year-old you could explain out-of-control gambling in this way: 'It's like when you have a bag of sweets and you just can't stop eating them all up. You might not even want them all really but you still can't stop. Then you feel ill. Well, Daddy's in a real fix. He has an illness that makes him gamble more than he really wants to. Then he feels a lot worse because he's gambled so much and he's lost all his money. So he gambles some more because he thinks it will make him feel better – but it doesn't.'

  Emphasize the compulsion factor. Most older children know what addiction means. They know it's like an illness. They also need to know that someone who's addicted cannot get out of it without help. It may also need to be made clear that it's not catching or hereditary. Don't let them think that if they gamble at all, they will become addicted. Tell them that most people gamble responsibly and get a lot of fun out of it.

  Answer any questions truthfully.

  Q 'Will he get better?'
  A 'I don't know. That's up to him. If he gets help, he will.'
  Q 'Why does he keep shouting at you?'
  A 'That's part of his illness. He doesn't want to argue with me. He can't help it. He still loves me, and he still loves you.'
  Q 'You're very nasty to him sometimes. Why?'

51

A 'That's because I badly want him to get help and if I'm nice to him all the time he won't get help. Getting help is the only way he'll stop gambling. When he stops gambling, he'll be much happier and so will we.'

- *Try not to lose control.* This will really worry the children. While your gambling husband is losing control all over the place, you are their only security. Since it will be difficult – well-nigh impossible, in fact – never to show any anger in front of the children or within earshot, talk about it afterwards with them. Don't hide from them the fact that you are under a lot of stress but reassure them that you can cope with it.

- *Go along to a Gam-Anon meeting* before you reach the stage of feeling you can't cope any longer. Let the children and your husband see that getting help is a good idea and it works.

As far as coping is concerned, it doesn't stop when the gambler eventually goes for help. Family dynamics will be greatly changed now that the gambler has stopped being the 'bad boy' of the family and is doing his best to change. Whereas before the child was alongside his mother in coping with the 'bad boy', now the focus of his parents is entirely on each other and on the 'good boy's' struggles to stay good. The child is now in danger of being sidelined and could easily start to feel abandoned. Don't let this happen. Include him or her in all the family activities – and make sure there *are* plenty of family activities and not just outings for mother and father.

So far, we've considered only the happy ending to a wife's second option – taking the risk of changing from 'mother' to 'wife'. This was Linda's choice and, as we see, all turned out well. Her husband began to grow up, take responsibility for himself and look on her as an equal partner – his wife – and no longer as the forgiving, all-tolerant 'mother'.

What was the risk she took, and what would have happened if her refusal to play the 'mother' role had failed in its purpose? Katie took this risk too – this is her story.

When we married, Henry was seriously rich. He'd been working as a financial adviser for about ten years, moving up and up and getting huge salaries and commissions and perks. He was very much the man-about-town while he was a bachelor so, naturally, he gambled like the rest of them. Don't ask me how it all worked but I know he gambled on the money markets as well as gaming at casinos. Whenever we went abroad he'd search out a casino and spend most of his time there.

I think he loved me at first. I'd been a model and gave it up when we married. I just wanted to devote my time to being his wife and he adored having me on his arm and seeing the other men envying him. But gradually, we went out together less and less and he never fancied entertaining at home. He spent more and more time gambling and I first realized he was losing, losing, losing when he traded in his beloved Porsche for a second-hand Granada and started talking about moving to the country. I thought he meant a second home but – no – there I was in this draughty old farm cottage while he amused himself in the week at a little *pied-à-terre* in the City. He was very vague about his doings in the week but I knew it would be gaming or gambling – he didn't really have any other thoughts in his head.

I really was the good little wifey, waiting on Friday nights in a bright pinny for him to come home to a hot meal and a relaxing time within whiffing distance of the cows. So OK, funds began getting very low indeed and I found masses of unpaid bills in an old tin trunk he kept at the cottage, but I said nothing and just soothed his fevered brow on the rare occasions he came down to the cottage in a foul temper.

The balloon went up when he turned up mid-week with apparently all his worldly goods in a friend's Range Rover. 'What's up?' I said. 'Got the sack,' he said, not looking at me. 'And a golden handshake?' I said. 'Don't be so silly,' he said and pushed past me to the drinks cabinet.

Well, I put my foot down then. I'd been turning a blind eye all this time, wanting to spare his rocky ego but I wormed it all out of him in the end. While I'd been fossilizing among the cows he'd been gaily getting rid of all his money and whatever of mine he could get his hands on, the London flat sold, the cottage mortgaged to the hilt, no car, no pension, lots of debts and absolutely nothing to live on.

After that, everything happened so quickly. I'd lost all respect for him – but I still loved him quite a lot, certainly enough to have a go at making it to the shore together – you know, sink or swim. He'd begged me not to leave him. He said he couldn't manage alone. I was all he had, etc., etc. He was in tears. I said OK, I'd stay on condition that he either stopped gambling straight away or got some kind of help to stop. I said I'd do all the bill-paying, clear the debts and so on.

By this time I'd decided to go back to modelling – I'd been in touch with my old agency and I knew I could be a high earner again. In return he had to find a job locally, stay away from every sort of gambling and pay a third of his earnings for his 'lodgings' at home. We weren't making love at all during this time – it just wasn't on – so it was more like a landlady-lodger arrangement, or a paying guest. I was really tough but I knew we could do it if he stayed tough too.

But he didn't. He hated every bit of it. He found a job in an estate office but the market had gone completely flat so all he did was stare out of the window and go out and measure up homes that wouldn't sell in a million years. I used to go up to London quite a lot and I had a few foreign trips too, but I kept to the bargain and used all I earned to pay off our debts.

I began to smell a rat when I sensed someone else had been in the cottage while I was away. You know how women get this sixth sense when somebody else has used your kitchen or your car? I knew it wasn't Henry because he just bought packaged, precooked stuff from the supermarket while I was away. This was different – someone had used the casserole dish and the garlic press. When I found a bottle of Madame Rochas toilet water in the bathroom I had no doubts – he had another woman and she'd been staying with him in my home.

I taxed him – 'What did you expect?' he said. 'You were treating me like garbage, like a naughty little boy and now I've got someone who loves me and respects me and what's more *she doesn't mind if I gamble* . . .' I asked him if she didn't mind paying off all his debts as well and he said, 'No, she doesn't mind. She'll pay off the lot and put me up at her house – much better lodgings there than here, swimming-pool, bathroom of my own, marvellous nosh, rivers of wine, the lot – and she never nags like you do . . .'

So I lost him to a different 'mummy' who would let him go on being a little boy. It hurt a bit but I felt better when I saw the woman in question – she was much older than him and looked like the side of a house. He'd kept his looks – just – and he could still turn on the charm, but not for me. I've kept the cottage on for weekends but I've got this smashing boyfriend, Georgie, and we live in town where he runs a chain of launderettes. He's not madly rich but he denies me nothing. He hates gambling and loves drinking. Sometimes he goes OTT but I've no worries . . . not yet.

What Katie did was to risk turning from mother to wife and trying to get Henry to play his part in the process. He couldn't make it, and had to turn to someone who would go on propping him up and feeding his addiction. The marriage ended – which was just as well since Katie would surely have destroyed herself while trying to reconstruct the Henry she thought she'd married.

6
Help

A number of different forms of treatment for problem gamblers have been tried over the years. With some of them you wonder why gamblers ever submitted themselves to the 'cure'. One treatment was aversion therapy in the form of electric shocks. Its aim was to break the usual behaviour cycle of the off-course betting man:

- he comes home having lost all his money
- he shows remorse and promises to stop
- he makes a selection of 'sure bets' from the paper next day
- he gets hold of some money
- he goes to the betting shop and bets until it closes.

The shock was administered while the gambler was studying form and making his choice of potential winners. In one study of the treatment, out of the 14 compulsive gamblers who were offered it – all were men who bet off-course on dogs and horses – two refused treatment, four ended treatment after a few sessions, five stopped gambling, and had still stopped after a year, and three ended up in prison.

Other behavioural treatments had their day. One was 'stimulus satiation' which meant that the gambler was hospitalized and flooded with gambling material like racing commentaries blaring out non-stop, racing posters all over the walls and the hospital staff allowed only to talk about gambling. The results are recorded as 'For four out of every five patients, gambling ceased to be a major problem.'

Critics of these behavioural and psychological approaches pointed out that very few psychiatrists and psychologists had ever been inside a betting-shop. They were out of touch with gamblers and gambling, it was claimed, and could not, therefore, fathom the best way into the closed circle of the addict's world.

One very promising treatment was directed at solving the problems arising from gambling with practical help. This, it was hoped, would steer the gambler away from one of the strongest fantasies in his 'dream world', that gambling itself will solve his problems. This programme had four phases and, as we shall see, is very similar to the practical part of Gamblers Anonymous' programme of recovery:

- Legal advice, budgeting, repayment plans.
- Returning to work.
- Marriage guidance.
- Group therapy with other problem gamblers.

However, all these treatments had their drawbacks and failures – the main one being a lack of commitment on the part of many of the gamblers who were embarking on the treatment. There seemed to be something missing – a touch of mysticism, a spiritual element, a magic spell, something 'other' that would keep addicts committed to changing their ways. It wasn't until the advent of Gamblers Anonymous (GA) and its sister organization, Gam-Anon, for the partners of problem gamblers, that people interested in the problem began to get an idea of what the missing ingredient might be. However, before looking at GA's way of helping the problem gambler, we'll see what help there is for his hard-pressed partner. It is she, after all, who has the crucial task of getting him to accept help and, without that, all could be lost.

Help for the gambler's partner

You've done quite well with all the tactics suggested in Chapter 5; you've shared your problems with some good friends; you've rung the Samaritans when you've felt low; you've seen your GP and he's referred you for some counselling and given you some medication; you are now beginning to see light at the end of the tunnel. Your addicted partner is still declaring he doesn't need help and he can stop gambling any time he wants – though his denials are getting a little fainter and less convincing. You're coping but only just. So now is the time to get some support and fellow-feeling by going to Gam-Anon.

What can Gam-Anon do for you, besides offering comfort and support from others in the same boat? Overall, it can help you understand and accept this compulsion, or illness that your partner has. That means a lot with a problem that's so little understood by the general public and probably by your own family and friends as well. However, even more important is what it can do for you personally in what appears to be an endless exercise of banging your head against a brick wall. Gam-Anon can:

- free you from a sense of hopelessness
- free you from a feeling of failure
- free you from guilt feelings

- give you understanding
- give you companionship and friendship
- bring you back to a normal way of relating to others (not always battling against problems)
- set you on your feet to plan your life and make decisions.

As the stories of other members' lives unfold, you'll be able to tie it in with your own experience and recognize the same well-worn dodges and deceptions practised by the hardened gambler. You'll learn both the daily tactics and also the long-term strategies for coping with your husband's problem, and gradually get round to the crucial question of how to motivate him to get help.

Most importantly, members of Gam-Anon learn to help each other, so that new members coming into the group are supported in their turn. Gam-Anon wives often continue to come to meetings long after their partners have joined Gamblers Anonymous and have been off gambling for years. Members of both organizations are great at passing on the help they've had.

The main thing the new Gam-Anon member learns to do is to give up trying to control her husband and striving to stop his gambling. While she insists on being 'in charge', he can avoid responsibility for his problems and put it all on her.

'You'll never get your act together,' she's saying, especially when she's treating him as useless or bawling him out. 'It's all down to me, as usual.' This is the game of 'You disabled child, me marvellously managing martyred mum', and he will play as long as she will play. So she needs to learn how to become a non-player.

If this is the situation you're in, being a non-player in his games basically means playing for yourself for a change. Try not to think of yourself as half of a unit of two but as a whole, separate person who lives alongside another whole, separate person, not melded into one with him. Get some outside interests. Build up your confidence so that whatever your partner does, you don't always see it as a strike against you. The thing about addicts is that they are all the time too much *for* themselves to be *against* anyone else.

Many a gambler's wife is so hurt by the deception, the broken trust, the indications that he no longer cares for anyone but himself, that she easily comes to believe that he is doing all these dreadful things *in order* to hurt her. It is never like that. He does all these dreadful things *in order to gamble* and to offload his guilt about gambling – and that's the whole story. Hang on to this truth because it makes it easier to be loving.

There is a final step which, according to GA's experience, has to be reached before the problem gambler is ready to accept help – his personal rock-bottom. In the words of Gordon Moody, founder of GA in the UK:

> A 'rock-bottom' is a frightening personal crisis that temporarily stops his fall and leads him to look around for help. It is not an absolute bottom but a ledge. You can help him while he is on that ledge . . . Nagging, badgering, bullying will not help, but if you try to show him that there is a way back up again and that he can take it and that you will give him all the support he wants while he is trying, you may succeed.

Everyone recognizes that all this is asking an enormous amount of a woman who is, at this stage, worn out by the demands put upon her by a sick and selfish partner and whose love and respect for him has been well and truly buried by the dance he's led her over the past few years. This is why everyone involved with the recovery of gamblers is at pains to say that a partner who can't manage this superhuman task of back-up need never feel guilty or ashamed.

The pity is that for many problem gamblers, the arrival on the ledge comes too late – they have already lost their partners, along with everything else that matters to them, and there is no back-up in their personal lives to sustain them through the GA programme. Sadly, the evidence is that gamblers without this personal support are much less likely to stick with the GA programme or seek any other form of help.

Help for the compulsive gambler

Gamblers Anonymous is the 24-hour nationwide service for people who seriously want to stop gambling. It started in Los Angeles in 1957, now has hundreds of groups across the world and was launched in the UK in 1964 by Methodist minister, Gordon Moody. From his interest in social issues and the real lives of ordinary people, the Reverend Moody had developed an extraordinary understanding of problem gamblers. This was based on talks with people associated with gambling from all walks of life. A lot of his talking was done with gamblers sent to prison for crimes committed to fund their habit, mostly petty larceny, breaking and entering, etc. – no bullion robbers they.

He discovered that they experienced the same 'buzz' from gambling as they had from being 'on the job', i.e. while committing a crime. Both activities gave them the excitement of 'getting away with it', the same nervous tension – 'Will I be caught or not? Will I lose or win?' They were trapped, he realized, in two continuous circles – one of arousal, suspense and excitement which encompassed the gambling activity itself; the second, with the same ingredients, covering all the activities necessary to get money for gambling.

This led him to tease out the difference between the heavy gambler and the problem gambler and to arrive at the conclusion that the latter is so obsessed with gambling that he interprets the whole of life as a similar risk-taking exercise. He stakes everything – home, job, family, peace of mind, self-respect and his very life. He is a risk-taker through and through, doomed to go round and round the two circles, completely out of control and with no idea of how to stop the motion.

What Gordon Moody also realized was that anything that could somehow intrude into these circles and start the problem gambler on his way out of his obsession was going to be his only lifeline. He needed someone or something to stop his fast-rotating world for him and let him get off. Moody illustrates this with an account of the arrest of one of the imprisoned gamblers he talked with:

> He had had to leave home again because of the problems created by his gambling and for a few weeks he engaged in gambling and petty crime, sleeping rough. He was going nowhere, but the way he was driven through it all gave it a fearful purpose. . . . At last he spoke of the policeman's hand on his shoulder. It was a relief, he said, such a relief to stop: to stop the whole thing, the one continuous and inclusive activity of gambling.

Gamblers Anonymous is the equivalent of the policeman's hand on the shoulder. Going to the first meeting can give the gambler the same sense of relief. He doesn't have to stay on his treadmill for ever and ever. The world is being stopped for him – he can step off. However, stepping off and starting the climb back to safety will take a great deal of personal effort and commitment.

That's perhaps one of the reasons why GA's success rate is not measured, another being their focus on the individual member rather than on statistics. One estimate is that 40 per cent of people going to their first meeting stay on the programme until they have not only stopped gambling but consider themselves well clear of any temptation to gamble again. The result is many members who have been 'cured' for several years but stay on to make sure and to help new members coming into the group.

Many first-time attenders drop out because their problems tend to seem quite light compared with the heavy disasters recounted by other members, so they feel as if they don't really need help or are actually 'cured' and that first meeting turns out to be their last.

There are some drawbacks to GA's methods and ethos, as seen by some people specializing in gambling addiction. One is the expectation of complete abstinence from gambling, even from buying lottery tickets. Possibly this is hard to live up to but it's in line with Alcoholics Anonymous' ban on any alcoholic drink whatsoever, not just a hair of the dog that caused the addiction, and it appears to make sense.

Another objection is to the concept of addictive gambling as an illness – some experts would rather it was seen as a personality disorder or a behavioural problem. Personally I can't see that it matters, since the concept of illness is clearly helpful to the gambler and his family and it works as a basis for GA's methods. Finally, many people think it's a pity that GA doesn't advertise. The value of advertising is debatable, except as a hook for fund-raising. Even then, it can put up as many backs as it attracts backers. What GA and other help organizations in the gambling field ought to be getting, of course, is some of the money assigned to good causes from the Lottery.

How does Gamblers Anonymous work?

The basis of GA's help is a twofold recovery programme. The first part is a number of practical steps which the gambler is urged to take on the principle that, if you change the behaviour, the personality will change. These steps include being completely honest about the problem and its spin-offs with family, friends, employer and, if applicable, the police; sorting out the financial mess and starting regular repayment of debts; facing up to and mending broken relationships and, running all through, guarding oneself constantly against a return to gambling.

The second part is a 12-step recovery programme aimed at changing the inner man. Its keynotes are honesty, humility and the recognition of 'a Power greater than ourselves' to which the gambler is going to submit his will and his life. Later in the list come references to God, and contact with God through prayer.

This religious note has made some people uneasy, particularly if they simply do not believe that there is any supernatural power watching over us and, if there were, it would be a complete denial of personal responsibility to hand over one's life and one's will to it. This, in essence, is the humanist stance of many individuals and agencies who are in the business of helping people and who, in the perceived absence of any power 'out there' which can be relied on to guide us and care for us, see it as imperative that we love and care for each other, not in the name of any deity but in the name of humanity.

The irony is that this is precisely what GA does. In spite of the programme's appeal to a greater power, actually identified in some of the 12 steps as God, the philosophy behind its work is that our salvation lies in mutual support and brotherly love.

In fact, GA emphasizes that it is not a religious organization and is open to all comers, of any faith or none, the only requirement for membership being 'the desire to stop gambling'. To the words 'Power' and 'God', where they appear in the 12 steps, is added the phrase 'of our own understanding', thus leaving members to interpret the spiritual element of the programme in their own way.

There is a further table of 12 points which is to do with the purpose and day-to-day running of the organization and its self-governing, self-financing groups. It stresses unity, anonymity and the non-professional status of GA. It is apolitical, has 'no opinion on outside issues' and avoids public controversy, self-promotion and any kind of sponsorship or public fund-raising. Its one primary purpose in any interaction with the general public is to 'carry its message to the compulsive gambler who still suffers'.

Recovery is a slow, one-day-at-a-time process. If, like the alcoholic who can say, 'I didn't drink today', the recovering gambler can say, 'I didn't have a bet today', then he's considered to be getting somewhere – though he won't be getting somewhere fast. There may be stumbles and set-backs along the way, but the programme goes on – there's no hurry.

What happens at Gamblers Anonymous meetings?

I was at one of the open meetings of a local GA group in a medium-sized town in South-East England. (Open meetings are not like the regular meetings of GA at which members concentrate on helping each other. They are a potential member's first contact with GA and he or she could just sit and observe, as I did, if they wished.) It was held in rather a smart meeting room in the public library. About thirty of us sat in the usual 'town hall' stacking chairs in red plastic. The room was warm and very brightly lit, with a table and a lectern on one end, facing the chairs. Also, for later, there were some coke bottles and packets of biscuits on a side-table.

There was a friendly feel in the room. Everyone smiled at everyone else. A man I'd met in the lift introduced me to some of the other people who came into the room. They were mixed ages – ranging from one smartly dressed man in his fifties to a young Asian in jeans who looked around 20. When the seats were pretty well all occupied, a slight man in glasses welcomed us in a thick Scots accent.

'If some of you can't understand what I'm saying – tough!' he said. We all laughed – the others because it was probably a standard joke, me because it told me the evening was going to be lighter than I'd expected. He referred to his notes and said, 'I now call upon Don.'

A stocky man walked to the lectern and said, 'I'm Don and I'm a compulsive gambler.' The rest of us chorused, 'Hullo, Don'. As one man after another went up to the lectern, they all started like this. 'I'm Phil and I'm a compulsive gambler.' 'Hullo, Phil.' 'I'm John and I'm a compulsive gambler.' 'Hullo, John.'

Even the ones who were later presented with pins to celebrate two, five or even seven years without a single wager still announced themselves as 'compulsive gamblers'. The point is that no one is ever considered to be an ex-gambler or a former gambler. They're all gamblers who didn't gamble yesterday or today and don't intend to gamble tomorrow.

Don went on to tell us the horror story of his slide into degradation and debt because of his gambling addiction. His first marriage broke down; he lost his home, wife and three sons; he lost his job as a gas fitter; when he started up his own taxi firm with a mate, he drove that into bankruptcy by gambling away the profits; he was still gambling and on a winning streak when he met Eva. Not long afterwards she became his second wife.

Eva knew that Don liked a flutter but not the extent to which he gambled. She couldn't understand where all the money was going, nor where he went day after day when it came out that he had no job. After months of dreadful scenes and Don's refusal to say anything about himself – 'He just pulled down the blinds,' Eva said later – he at last broke down and confessed. It took Eva another four years to persuade him to get help and go to GA. Eight years ago, after gambling compulsively for 28 years, he went. Don hasn't had a bet for seven years – but he's still a compulsive gambler.

The other GA members speaking that night had similar tales to tell. Ron, in his twenties, had robbed his parents to pay for gambling; Amin had taken money out of his young daughter's savings; John had lost his job in a bank through an attempt to divert some clients' money. All of them described families in conflict and lives in ruins. Some had made suicide attempts; others had tried to 'go missing' and failed. They all found, in the old cliché, that they couldn't run away from themselves.

They all paid tribute to the rescue operation of GA, said that from the moment they began going to meetings, their lives had changed. They spoke of recovering their self-esteem and confidence, of ending their 'sickness' and of needing only humility, courage and honesty to get back on the right track.

After the gamblers had spoken it was the turn of the wives. What struck me most was how very strong they all were. They weren't strident or bossy, just determined that their men would stop gambling and never slip back. No goody-goody frumps they, either – they were all incredibly young and attractive.

They said how much easier it was when the gambler had confessed and they knew what they were dealing with – and they all said it had taken years of suspicion and arguments to get to that point. Babs, for example, had lived for four years with the knowledge of Jack's habit but was unable to get him to go for help. In the end, by going to Gam-Anon, she'd learned from other wives how to get him through the door to a GA meeting – and they never looked back.

I came away from the meeting cheered and impressed. I'd expected to meet a sad bunch of withdrawn down-and-outs engrossed in justifying all their past mistakes. Instead, here was this crowd of smart, aimiable, outgoing men and women with a kind of evangelistic fervour about their commitment to change and to their fellow members of GA.

I'm telling you about this meeting because so many gamblers and their partners reach the desperate stage where they think nothing and no one can help. They get to rock-bottom, all hope and money gone, and believe that there's no way back. Well, there is.

When the compulsive gambler is a woman

We noted in Chapter 3 that female gambling addicts are fairly rare but that we expect to see more since the Lottery and scratch cards have proved so popular with females of all ages. Can we, however, expect them to get help?

When GA started, almost no women presented themselves for help. It was thought that, as time went by and gambling grew to be seen as an illness, for which the gambler needed help, rather than as a moral lapse he was too weak-willed to overcome, more and more female addicts would be willing to admit to their problem and get help for it. This is what happened at Alcoholics Anonymous as problem drinkers were gradually recognized as sick rather than sinful and women alcoholics felt less ashamed and 'unwomanly' and more willing to seek help. As a result, the membership of Alcoholics Anonymous hovers around equal numbers of men and women.

This is still not the case with gambling addiction. The reasons for this, as far as the research goes – which is not far – seem to be:

- A gambling woman who is economically dependent on her husband keeps the mounting problems and debts a secret from him right up until the point of no return. She fears discovery far more than she fears financial ruin.
- When the crisis comes, help for her is the last thing on anyone's mind. In an atmosphere of shock and rejection, all her husband's efforts are turned to salvaging the family fortunes.
- When a wife and mother gambles excessively it has a much more disastrous effect on a family. When father gambles, mother holds everything together. When mother gambles, not only the financial situation but also the day-to-day life of the family crumbles into chaos. Again, any help available is focused at first on the main victims – the virtually motherless children.
- It has been found that men are much less supportive of a partner who gambles than women are in a similar situation. They often react to the wife's problem as a gigantic betrayal, something far beyond their understanding or willingness to forgive.
- Financially independent women who gamble to excess have as much or as little need as the gambling bachelor to curb their habit or to feel in need of help. If they have no family or other supportive network, and if they don't get help, they will go on gambling until they end up in prison or on the streets as bag women or prostitutes.

One woman's story is typical of many. Delia and her husband ran a thriving garden centre on the outskirts of an East Anglian town. All went well while they were struggling to build up the business from a garden shed and a greenhouse on a one-acre site. But as it grew successful, Delia became bored, restless and vulnerable to anything that would relieve her boredom.

> When we could afford someone else to do all the ordering and bookwork and so on, which used to be my job, I really had time on my hands. Vic still had his role. He knew all about plants and trees and garden planning and he was in his element. He was very popular whereas I knew all the customers who clustered round him were

wondering how the heck he came to have such a boring, dowdy wife. I never had any confidence, often wondered myself why such an exciting chap had married me.

He thought he was doing me a terrific kindness by getting staff in to take over everything I did for the business, so I can't blame him. But it was a disaster. I'd never made friends locally. I often wished we'd had some children in the early days when we thought we couldn't afford them. Vic never bothered about not having a family, but I did – sometimes I wondered what I was for. I couldn't see that I had any purpose really.

At the other end of town where it wasn't so posh, there was a bookie's office where I used to go in the old days once a year, just for the Grand National. I thought I'd try it again for the ordinary race meetings and soon I was nipping over there almost daily. I didn't have any money of my own. I was regularly emptying our joint bank account, which was for household things, and then selling my clothes and possessions and even some furniture and pictures to go on gambling.

Then I started taking money from the till at the garden centre and that was a big mistake because there was no way I could cover up. The accountant pointed out to Vic that things weren't matching up. Suspicion fell on one of the assistants at the centre and I let that potter along for a while. Then Vic started doing something he hadn't done for years, which was to look at me and listen and see what my life was like. He put a lot of twos and twos together and said, 'Are you all right? Is something wrong?'

I couldn't admit to the gambling. I said I was depressed, which was partly true, and didn't know what I was doing half the time. He marched me off to the doctor for some tablets and treated me like a china doll for about three weeks.

Soon I was back to my normal self, gambling all hours. This time, Vic wasn't fooled. He was very angry and said I had to stop and that I must go for help. It was no use denying I was hooked but I reckoned I didn't need help, I could fight it myself.

Vic couldn't take any more. He said I was ruining him and the business. He'd had a girlfriend for a long time, he told me. He bought me a tiny terraced house the other side of town – ironically, it was near the bookie's office – gave me a sort of pension and started a divorce. The girlfriend's living with him now and I just gamble as much as I want. It's getting a bit hard though. I still get so depressed. I keep selling stuff, there's not much left.

Sometimes I think about moving up to live with my mother but she thinks I'm rubbish – always has – so that wouldn't really work. Other times I feel like killing myself. I ring up the Samaritans a lot. The lovely lady there keeps asking me if I wouldn't like to join Gamblers Anonymous and get help. But I don't know. I don't like the idea of more people knowing how rubbishy I am. I don't see how anyone could accept me, not the way I am now. I might as well stay like this and just keep out of everyone's way until it's time to go.

Delia's dependence on her husband possibly made her addiction a lot worse – she had no means of raising her badly bashed self-esteem. For independent women who are earning their own living, it might be less easy to be drawn into addiction and perhaps easier to get help if they did become addicted.

There's a reason not to be too optimistic about this, however. By acquiring independence, more and more women have joined men in the army of the insecure, stressed, anxious, debt-laden citizens of an increasingly violent, uncaring society. They have therefore become no less vulnerable to the escape into fantasy offered by addictions of all kinds. So the need for help is not going to get less for either sex, and the message for a woman who's in a gambling trap is the same as for a man – get help.

7
Recovery

When your gambling partner has finally faced up to his problem, has gone to Gamblers Anonymous and is settled into regular meetings, that's not quite time for you to relax and breathe a sigh of relief. You will find that he's spending almost as much time and energy on being 'cured' as he was on the gambling. The road back gradually takes over as the main preoccupation of his life, and the family will have to accept with good grace his absences at meetings and his still rather switched-off presence in the home.

You may be faced with a certain amount of moodiness and withdrawal symptoms for some time. At the meetings with fellow recoverers he will have been constantly brought back to reality and to such unwelcome home truths as the fact that his problem is not money, or the loss of his job, or his failing marriage, but gambling. In gradually accepting these truths at the meeting, he will be buoyed up by the general air of hope, and by the evidence that other gamblers, once far worse off than he is now, have pulled through.

There will also be a kind of honeymoon period after a gambler has admitted his problem and is getting help. His partner may have greeted his confessions with relief – even the enormous debts – because she was suspecting far worse. They are perhaps already on the same side again instead of enemies and now he has all the GA group members on his side too.

Everyday life at home, however, soon puts an end to the honeymoon period. This is the base from which he ventured out on all his former gambling activities. It is the take-off point for the routine that carried him along from one 'buzz' to the next. So it is here that he comes up against the nitty-gritty. He can see how much his life has already changed and how much more it has to change before he's over the hump.

How has his life changed?

- His former routine is in tatters, causing disorientation.
- He misses his old haunts – the bookies, the casino, the race-track.
- He misses his gambling companions.
- Now that his money affairs are out in the open, he's worried about debts.
- No longer able to hide everything from you, he's feeling ashamed and guilty.

- If there are serious practical problems to be faced – e.g. a pending court appearance, threatened repossession of the home – he won't be able to run away from them as of old.
- He may be having grave doubts that he can make it through the recovery programme.
- His self-esteem is still very low, his pride has had to give way to humility and he's feeling insecure – but there's no escape into gambling.
- Most of all, he misses the gambling – the only thing he lived for.

You can understand, I expect, how fragile his ego is at this stage and how lonely and afraid he's feeling. He'll also be restless and bored. He has lost something that was his whole life in terms of time spent on it and in terms of occupying all his thoughts and feelings. What can you do to lessen his pain and help his recovery? Here are some of the things he will be feeling and doing and the most helpful ways you could respond.

How you can help

- *He* will be only too aware that he has hurt you and damaged the family and that you now occupy the high moral ground.
- *You* will help him most if you don't press these points. Don't act as if, in supporting him, you're doing him a favour. That's not the case. You are doing something much more important – backing the family's survival.
- *He* is also aware that this is his last chance. He has reached rock-bottom and the only way is up – or a bleak, lonely, hopeless future.
- *You* know that if he gives up and returns to gambling, that's the end of your relationship. Don't hammer the point but don't let it disappear.
- *He* may still hope that you will fix the nuts and bolts of his recovery for him – make a debt repayment plan, contact his creditors, etc.
- *You* mustn't. And you don't need to. These are all his responsibilities now. With help from GA members, he can do the planning and decision-making himself. But you should expect him to keep you in the picture and to get your agreement to the major decisions. If he wants you to, you could go with him to meet his bank manager or creditors or anyone else involved – but let him do the talking.
- *He* may be tempted to have a bet if he has 'spare' money in his pocket or at his disposal. He may even be afraid of this temptation.
- *You* can help him, with his agreement, by seeing to all the household bills yourself so that he has enough cash with him only to cover his personal expenses for the day.

- *He* will be trying very hard to be honest and truthful with you.
- *You* must try very hard to believe him and trust him. This will not be easy after all the years of lies and deception. It's not easy for him either. From being a compulsive liar who comes to believe his own lies he now has to present the plain, unvarnished truth about himself and every detail of his life to you, to GA members and to the world. It will take time.

Filling the gap

For a recovering adult gambler, and even more so for a young gambler, one of the main challenges is to see that he has some other interests to fill the enormous space that was occupied by gambling and then, for a while, by the recovery programme. Some experts who treat addicts suggest that he might even need to find some other neurosis as strong as an addiction, but less harmful, to ease him off the dangerous addiction he's trying to get rid of.

Unfortunately, no one can think of a neurosis as strong as an addiction that isn't itself an addiction, nor think of an addiction that isn't ultimately dangerous. However, a fanatical attitude to a hobby or sport can be rewarding and not necessarily harmful.

One gambler I knew took up making model aeroplanes out of balsa wood. This looked promising – it was cheap, noiseless and kept him at home. But his wife couldn't take those chippings and shavings all over the place – which was strange when she'd put up with so much worse in his gambling days. Perhaps it was the last straw. Fortunately, his hobby had already worked its magic – he was laid-back enough to say, 'OK. Forget the balsa wood. I'll make plastic planes instead.' And so he did.

Because money will be tight for the first few years of recovery while the debts are being repaid, the interests that a recovering gambler can take up are rather limited. One family in which the father had been a compulsive gambler spent all their weekends flying kites when the weather was suitable and when it wasn't they sat together with audio tapes and video tapes and books and taught each other to speak Italian, ready for the holiday they were going to have in a few years.

If that sounds unbelievably virtuous and strong-minded, just think of the kind of life it was replacing, one to which they would all have quickly slipped back if they weren't determined enough. There was no kite-flying in those days, no family life involving all its members. The three children virtually grew into their teens without a father and the wife spent the years of her marriage bonded to an overgrown child who, unlike her real children, took all and gave nothing.

When a father's recovering, do your best to include the children in family events and outings and in discussions about what's going on. It will help them if you can explain that their father is getting better but it's hard work for him and takes a long time. Because of all the efforts the adults are putting into sorting out their lives, it can be easy for the children to feel cut out as much as when you were coping with the trauma of his gambling. When that was happening, the children certainly felt cut out by their father. This time they might feel that both parents are abandoning them.

Will he really get better?

Some wives wonder if anyone who fell so headlong into addiction in the first place could ever be strong enough to get free of its powerful hold and rebuild his life. Just how balanced and mature does a person need to be to go through the long, hard slog to recovery? The gambler himself often takes fright at what's expected of him – that's basically what drives a lot of GA recruits back to gambling after their decision to give it up. It's rather like someone with a minor condition finding that the treatment is going to make him a lot worse before it makes him better.

The point about the gambling 'cure', however, is that you really do need to be very bad indeed before you can accept the necessity for change. Significantly, many men who've ducked out of the first or second meeting of GA come back when things are much worse. They hadn't reached their rock-bottom. They weren't ready to change.

Supposing that, before he gambled or, at any rate, before it became compulsive, your partner was as normal as anyone else? (Which is not to say 100 per cent normal, by any means . . .) In that case, giving up gambling will probably restore him in time to his former state, with the added bonus of lessons learned and strengths gained. Supposing, instead, that he was low in self-esteem and emotional security to start with? This is highly likely since we saw in Chapter 3 that these characteristics are found to be shared in one degree or another by most problem gamblers. Can recovery not only make him better than his gambling self but also better than he was before he became addicted? Can any form of help improve on the original mould?

I believe it can. Any treatment, cure or recovery programme which gives a person insight into his 'sickness', and helps him to be responsible for himself and his actions, is going to send out a person more 'whole' than the one who came in. So it helps recovery if the problem gambler is basically a strong person, but it's not essential. It helps him to be strong, whether he started that way or not, if he has the right kind of help; loyal

70

support from someone who matters to him – and to whom *he knows* he matters; and something to fill that yawning gap where the gambling was.

Sometimes, the problem gambler is driven into a substitute compulsion as strong as the gambling. He may fling himself impatiently into repaying his debts, taking on several jobs at once, and pouring all his earnings into repayments, with the result that the sufferings of his wife and family are about the same as when he was gambling. When this happens, his fellow members at GA will help him to see what he's doing and persuade him to take things at a less hectic pace.

Patience and understanding

A great deal of the recovery programme is to do with handling tension and impatience but this, like everything else, can't succeed overnight. Perhaps the quality that the gambler and his partner need most is patience and the next in importance is an understanding of each other's difficulties. Pam describes what it's like to stand by while your partner climbs out of his addiction.

There wasn't one day went by all the time we were married that Steve didn't gamble. He kept his job all right but often it was a near thing. He was doing deliveries all over the South – some sort of office equipment in a light van – and he had plenty of opportunity to go to a betting-office or even a race-course on the way, especially if he had lots of different deliveries in one place.

This all came out later, by the way. All I knew at the time was that he had this job that took him away from home a lot of the time – even at weekends, he said – but didn't bring in much money.

He was found out when those mobile phones came in and the office could keep track of him. He had to lie more and more to account for the times when they couldn't get hold of him. He got the sack long before I knew anything about it. For weeks he was going off at the usual time and, of course, there was nothing strange about him turning up at all hours.

It took two years of terrible debts, arguments, a house move, losing all our friends, etc. before he went for help. He said that what he hadn't been able to face was the idea of any bet being his last. That was six months ago and now he says that actually stopping gambling wasn't the worst part – it was more of a big load off his back. What he finds hard is getting into the swing of anything else. He's started his own business mending cars – he was always good at that – but sometimes he's so depressed that he can't summon up the energy to do any work or tout for it.

He gets pills from the doc – they seem to be working as the depressions aren't so long or so bad. I worry a bit about him being at home on his own most days – he does some of his car work here, in the yard, or he might go to the customer's place if it's not a major job.

I work full-time, of course, otherwise we'd be sunk. Our son is off at college. He's a computer wizard. He never had a good word for his father in the old days but I think he respects him now for what he's trying to do. I've seen them in long conversations sometimes which never, ever happened when Steve was gambling.

That's the kind of change that makes me very happy. Another one is when I hear Steve whistling about the place. He never did that when he was gambling either, but I remember it from when we were first married and he was just going to the bookies once a week. He still whistles the same old tunes though, 'Beautiful dreamer' is his favourite. He's quite a softie really.

I just carry on as if everything was normal. I don't make a fuss of him and I don't put him down either. I just *expect* him to pull through and I often tell him I know he will. We don't have any social life together but, thank goodness, I have a lot of outings with the people at work. When Steve's better I'll have them all here for a party – they've been bricks through all our troubles. I don't know how anyone in my shoes could survive without friends.

At the minute he still feels ashamed about what he put me and the boy through. He's just keeping his head down, apart from going to his meetings. Give it another year or 18 months – he'll be all right, you'll see.

Some gamblers simply don't respond to the GA programme. This puts them in a dilemma because there's not much else in the way of specialized therapy or self-help for people with this particular problem. They could go for general counselling – either through their GP or by contacting the British Association for Counselling, details in Chapter 12. For their debt problems, they can get free help from their local Citizens Advice Bureau and for their marriage or relationship worries, they can contact Relate (marriage guidance). The nearest centre will be listed in the local phone book.

What if he can't stop gambling?

This is something you have to think about. The collective history of addicted gamblers is by no means a record of happy endings in the sense that they've all stopped gambling and never looked back. However, the gamblers who can't give up are not necessarily unhappy endings. There's a temptation to think of them as absolute failures because the GA programme, like that of Alcoholics Anonymous, aims at total abstinence. This undoubtedly works for most problem gamblers but there are other theories about recovery which recognize the possibility that compulsive gambling can be controlled and the gambler diverted to responsible, moderate betting. The father of a 20-year-old compulsive gambler who still lived at home describes his son's partial recovery.

I have to admit that I felt responsible for Alan's problem. When he was 18 and out of a job, I took him along to the bookies to cheer him up. As luck would have it, he won and was immediately hooked. I gave up the weekly gamble myself but for him it was too late.

It's been hell for the last four years. He's wanted to stop, deep down, but couldn't make it. He stole from us, then apologized, paid us back and did it again. He had a job for a while in a corner store but he continually had his hand in the till and ended up in court. Mary and I were desperate. We loved him but he was ruining my retirement and he had no prospect of getting his own place and leaving us in peace. He appeared to have no interest in the home or us – he was just taking all he could get and giving us nothing in return. When he wasn't out gambling or thieving, he'd be shut up in his room, only coming out for meals.

Things got so bad that I was on the verge of a nervous breakdown and went to my GP who referred me for counselling. It turned out that I felt so guilty about starting Alan on gambling that I was more or less paralysed by it – I just couldn't make any move to help him or stop his problem affecting us.

This was a breakthrough. We made a contract with Alan – if he stuck to certain rules we would support him all the way and he could go on living at home. If he broke any rules *for a second time* he would be out and he'd have to go and find a home for himself. (This wasn't as drastic as it sounds because he'd often stayed for several days with a friend and could have moved in. But this was in a shabby bedsit – Alan described it as a 'tip' – in a run-down part of town. I've been along that road and you could really *smell* the poverty and squalor. Alan is rather fussy about his surroundings – a real old maid – so he certainly didn't relish the prospect of living there.)

Well, we stuck to the contract and so did he. Frankly, I think it was an enormous relief to him that he wasn't being expected to stop gambling altogether. If he slipped up, however slightly, I got really tough – something I'd never done before and he seemed to welcome it. He was like a kid really, any attention was better than none. I certainly had been much too tolerant and distant before.

He still lives at home but he has a part-time job in the local park and he's beginning to mix with non-gambling types, including females. We have hopes he'll marry and settle down one day. When we're gone, he'll have the bungalow, of course. We realize that perhaps he'll never stop gambling but at least it's under control now – there's none of the stealing and secrecy and the awful lies. And there are things to be thankful for – it could all have been a lot worse.

I asked Alan's father to tell me, first, what were the terms of the contract that worked so well for Alan and his parents and, second, what they felt they had to be thankful for about Alan's problem. After all, he was still a gambler and that was the root of all the other problems he had caused in the family. The rules in the contract were:

- The rules were not negotiable. Once agreed to, the contract was cast-iron.
- Alan had no access whatever to the parents' money – cash, credit cards, cheque-books, savings, etc. were all kept out of his way.
- Alan's father gave him a small weekly allowance – £5 to start with – which rose by £1 for every month that Alan stuck to the rules and stayed out of trouble. He was given no other money at all by anyone but he had his full keep at home, a fair-sized bedsit with TV, and friends were always made welcome.
- He did his own clothes-washing and ironing, the washing-up after breakfast every day and after the evening meal every other day. He made sandwiches for his own lunch, whether he was going to be out or in. He cooked the evening meal once a week, and catered for himself if his parents were out.
- He was responsible for certain household tasks like putting out the dustbin, getting in the fuel, cleaning his own room, the family car and the outside of the house-windows.
- His stake was limited to £3 on any one wager. If he won, he was still not to put more on. He kept a record of all his bets and he and his parents went over it together at the end of the day. Winnings were saved – the idea was that he never had more than his weekly £5 in his pocket when he went to the bookies. If he ran out of money before the end of the week – that was that. He couldn't bet again until pay-day unless he had *earned* extra money.
- He could make extra money for betting or saving by doing extra jobs

at home like decorating, gardening or spring-cleaning, or by getting any casual jobs he could find.

- His visits to the bookies were limited to short ones – up to two hours in the morning or the afternoon, not both – rather than the all-day sessions he'd been used to.

- He was to fill his non-gambling hours with a study course of his choice at the local college of further education and, twice a week, some sort of exercise of his choosing. (Alan chose to study car maintenance at the college and to play badminton at the local leisure centre.)

This was a pretty strict regime which one might have thought would bring Alan down to the status of a child with no control over his own life. However, as his father pointed out, a complete lack of control had been Alan's problem – he was unable to stop the gambling, the stealing, the lying and the self-destruction.

So any way back had to start with outside controls and then move on to self-control. Another point was that this regime gave Alan areas of total responsibility and ways he could contribute to the family. It also gave him opportunities to achieve all sorts of things – a sense of satisfaction, self-approval, a sense of pride, the feeling that he mattered to his parents, success at a chosen activity, and hope for the future.

One unforeseen advantage of the tight contract was that it slightly took the spontaneity out of the gambling experience and therefore something of the 'buzz' too. Alan's parents noticed, after a few months, that he wasn't using up the maximum permitted time for gambling and would sometimes miss a day altogether. After a while, it was clear that he was still very interested in gambling, but no longer compelled to gamble.

As for what Alan's parents saw as aspects of the problem they could be thankful for, this has to be a personal response, depending on a family's individual circumstances and the strength of the gambler's addiction. But the things they felt happy about could indicate where other parents might be able to count their blessings:

- They were thankful that Alan's problem wasn't drink or drugs. (This is a common response from a gambler's family.) At least his addiction wasn't damaging his physical health as alcohol and drugs do.

- The one potential threat to his physical health – starving in order to gamble – didn't apply. It was an undoubted plus that he lived at home and had regular meals.

- A gambling addiction is fortunately not 'messy' in the way that other addictions can be. Alan wasn't coming home smelling of drink,

75

falling about the place, vomiting on the carpet, groaning with pain next morning. Nor was he filling the house with cigarette smoke and fag-ends and posing a fire threat with all the paraphernalia of the addicted smoker. Most of all, he was not hooked into any life-threatening involvement with drugs – the addiction that causes the most worry to parents.

- Unlike alcoholism or drug abuse, the gambling habit doesn't make the gambler offensive or violent when he's under the influence. However, frustration at not having the means to gamble can lead to violence in the course of getting the funds. Alan's parents did not have this worry – they were subsidizing Alan's habit with just enough cash to keep him going at a moderate level.

- Alan's problems had not driven a wedge between his parents, as so often happens. They had become even more united in working out solutions and this united front was a help to Alan's sense of identity and security.

- Like many people involved with a gambler, Alan's parents had to admit that he had charm. He could make them laugh and he could make them feel good – he wasn't the type of bitter and twisted addict you come across in other contexts. This isn't to say that all gamblers are charming but in Chapter 3 I point to some reasons – notably their low self-esteem – why they are more likely to want to please people (except perhaps by giving up gambling) and to employ charm to that end than sufferers from other compulsions.

- Finally, Alan's parents hated the sin but continued to love the sinner. It was a blessing, they felt, that this had somehow got across to Alan so that he had never wanted to reject them and stage a walk-out. It was also a blessing that they had never felt like rejecting him, though often tempted. He would have been lost to them and to himself if he hadn't been helped to control his gambling.

What of the problem gambler who is lost long before he gets to the stage where recovery is possible? Well, recovery is always *possible*, however late the gambler comes for help – in fact, in the case of GA's help, the later he comes for it the better his chances of recovery. The only *impossible* situation is when the gambler fails to get any help at all. So there's no reason ever to give up hope or to stop plugging away at the need for help.

8

Young gamblers

Compulsive gambling and games playing by children and teenagers are comparatively new worries for parents and society. We had scarcely begun to realize the habit-forming potential of fruit machines before the enthralling video and computer games came along, closely followed by the National Lottery and its scratch cards. The latter, being available at your friendly neighbourhood newsagent to anyone aged 16 or over (and under 16 too, as we shall see), are recognized as the most lethal 'fix' of all on the gambling scene, and especially attractive to the young.

There are extreme views on all these forms of gambling and games playing, ranging from complacency to panic. None of these is justified. Youngsters can play the one-armed bandits, the arcade video space race and the latest 'shoot 'em up' game on their home computers without getting addicted. These forms of entertainment undoubtedly have their positive as well as their negative side. However, it makes sense to find out all you can about anything which has the power to override our natural barriers against excess – this is certainly something we do when it's drugs, sex, tobacco or alcohol which threaten our children's welfare. In the end, knowledgeable parents are the best defence against addiction that a child can have.

So what are the dangers for your children in gambling and games playing? How can you tell if your child is becoming addicted? If there is a problem, what can you do about it? Most important of all, how can we make sure that our children get the best out of these entertainments and avoid the worst?

Fruit machines

Many of today's adult problem gamblers were haunting the amusement arcades in the 1970s but no one at that time seemed to suspect that fruit machines could lead to a harmful addiction. In fact, fruit machines are still the only form of gambling legally open to people of any age, except for minor restrictions on under-16s playing in arcades (noted in Chapter 2 in the section on gaming machines). In public places other than arcades – in cafés, shops and motorway service areas, for example – there weren't and still aren't any restrictions at all. On the contrary, fruit machines were recently made even more appealing to young players when some machines which formerly issued tokens for a win were allowed to switch to cash prizes instead.

Worries began to surface in the late 1980s when stories appeared in the press about young gamblers who were driven to crime in order to fund their addiction. One young man of 23 had started playing fruit machines at the age of ten and had been imprisoned eight times for stealing. He estimated that he'd spent at least £100,000 on fruit machines during his gambling career. He described how he used to get up at 7 a.m., go straight to a café which had a machine and stay there until 7 p.m. when the café closed. Then he'd go out stealing in order to play next day. Another addict, a boy of 15, was reported to have stolen a brand new television set *from his own parents* and sold it for £20 to the owner of the chip shop where he played every day on the fruit machine.

The most horrific story, however, is of the 16-year-old in Wales who burgled the home of an 81-year-old grandmother to get money for fruit machines. His haul was £3.50 and as he left the house he set it on fire to avoid identification. The old lady died. The boy was found guilty of murder and ordered to be detained during Her Majesty's pleasure.

The boy's parents called on the government to ban youngsters from fruit machines. They told the court that he spent every penny he had on gambling – 'Nothing ever stayed in his pockets.' Although they had sometimes been able to drag him from shops and arcades, most of the time they couldn't control him. 'Unless something is done,' said the boy's mother, 'some other parents and some other kid will have to go through what we've been through' – not to mention, one might add, what the old lady and her family went through.

The head of Gwent CID noted that 'These machines are leading young kids to crime to feed their obsession' – a conclusion echoed by a piece of research on young gamblers which was published in the same week the boy was convicted. Estimating that there were 180,000 fruit machines currently in pubs, cafés, arcades and shops throughout the country, the study reported that one child player in ten spent more than £5 a session on the machines, with 7 per cent of players stealing to fund their habit and many more borrowing money or using school dinner money to play. It concluded that more than 1.8 million youngsters under 16 were playing in arcades at that time.

A psychiatrist explained how these machines can compel punters to go on playing far beyond what they can afford or control. He described their attraction as 'operant conditioning' – the more you play the more you want to play. This is based on the principle of the near miss. The first two reels often show the same symbol, needing only the third to be the same to win. Also the player can just see the lines below and above his line when it comes to rest and the symbols shown there are designed to make him think that next time he'll win. Extra controls (like the 'hold' button), messages, flashing lights and the sound of the wheels spinning round all encourage further play and raise the level of excitement.

Nevertheless, there was no great concern at the end of the 1980s by the government or experts. A Home Office report claimed, against most of the evidence, that youngsters were not spending substantial sums in amusement arcades nor turning to crime to finance their gambling. Critics of the report pointed out that the children were interviewed in the presence of their parents, breaking all the rules about confidentiality in this type of survey and raising doubts about the validity of their responses.

Soon, however, the alarm bells were ringing more persistently and from other directions. One reason for the renewed interest in problem gambling in the early 1990s was that it was fast becoming one of the favourite escapes from boredom and despair among the growing numbers of disaffected and rootless young people in the inner cities. Another reason was the rise of a new generation of psychologists and social workers who, on turning their attention to an under-studied area of society, were discovering that young people whose gambling is out of control are in considerable danger. Why is that?

Well, you don't have to be a psychologist to realize that addiction to anything is a much greater risk for children, teenagers and young adults than it is for older people. The young, by virtue of their youth and inexperience, are vulnerable to a take-over by any activity which promises instant gratification, easy rewards and pleasurable sensations. They are less likely to count the cost or to foresee the consequences of their gambling.

Another risk factor is the fact that the kind of obsession that leads to addiction – or, indeed, to perfectly healthy concentration on one sport or one hobby – is very strong in children and teenagers. Finally, children and adolescents are more prone to have irrational attitudes towards their activities and enthusiasms. In the case of fruit-machine gamblers, they tend to blame the machine for their losses and believe their wins are due to their own skill. They also tend to personalize the machine and set themselves up in competition against it, making the game a battle that the player feels he must win.

The young problem gambler, however, does not gamble primarily for the money that the machine occasionally returns to him. He may have started on the fruit machines for fun and to win but all the research shows that, by the time he's hooked, he gambles in order to gamble, end of story – except that soon he has to gamble *and steal* in order to gamble.

The official view that all this posed no dangers for the young was consistently questioned by a number of studies into the problem, notably those undertaken by Dr Mark Griffiths. In his latest book – *Adolescent Gambling* (Routledge, 1995) – he estimates that up to 6 per cent of young people may be addicted to fruit machines and that most of them are 'easily spending £100 a week' on them. He makes the point that it's difficult for parents to know what's going on.

Often the first families know about it is when children are in trouble over truancy or they have been picked up for shoplifting. There is a vicious circle whereby the more a child gambles, the more parents argue, the more a child wants to play the machines as an escape route.

How can you tell if your child is addicted to fruit machines? This can be difficult. Children can fool their parents for years if they really try. Also there is little visible evidence of gambling addiction, unlike cases where smoking, drugs or alcohol are the problem. Another difficulty is that the symptoms of addiction to gambling are often thought by parents to be signs of the usual changes in adolescence – lack of communication, mood swings, etc. So you must guard against blaming yourself for failing to spot trouble earlier – it really isn't easy. The following check-list should help you find out if there's a problem and whether or not your child needs help. Look for:

- a marked change in the child's overall behaviour – the sort of thing that perhaps only a parent will notice, like the outgoing child becoming reserved, or the even-tempered child becoming touchy
- the child's air of 'hugging a secret'. He or she always seems preoccupied, hardly ever communicates with the family, gives no account of movements or interests and offers much less eye-contact – in short, more detached
- unexplained free time
- constant shortage of money
- lack of friends
- no interest in school, work or family
- hungry – school-lunch money spent on gambling
- stealing.

Some more clues to help you – your child is more likely to become addicted to gambling if most of the following apply to him:

- he plays for money on other games
- he smokes and drinks alcohol
- he plays video games in arcades
- his parents gamble
- he plays alone
- he started gambling early – eight years or younger.

When you have identified the problem, what next? We will look at ways of responding to a young problem gambler and how to get help in the next chapter.

The Lottery and scratch cards

Although the National Lottery is recognized as addictive because of its mega-jackpot, it has no special appeal for the young because the interval between staking your money and knowing whether you've won or lost is too long. That's one of the reasons why scratch cards (or 'instants') are both highly addictive and also especially attractive to children and teenagers – and to the immature of all ages. The waiting time between stake and result is minimal – just the time it takes to rub a coin over a card and see if the same amount of money appears three times. Another inducement to buying them is that it's so easy to access the cards.

Although regional and local lotteries and instants have been popular all over the country for some time and have been very effective in raising money for charity, there has never been anything like the scale of Camelot's lottery and scratch card business and nowhere near the wide range of outlets and availability of tickets and cards. Altogether, scratch cards are probably the most user-friendly way of losing your money ever invented.

Another reason for their appeal to the young is that they are what's known as 'heart-stoppers' – they often show a near win. It's been said that, like the fruit machines, they are designed to do this. So, at £1 a go, the temptation is to go on and on until your money runs out.

Lottery tickets and scratch cards are not supposed to be sold to anyone under 16 but there is evidence that children as young as 12 were buying them in the first few months after they were launched. This evidence was uncovered by Children's Express, a children's charity which runs a news agency staffed by teenagers. It aimed to find out if retailers were sticking to the law and sent out a team of 12- to 15-year-old reporters to three groups of retail outlets – large stores and supermarkets, medium stores, and small stores and newsagents.

The results were that nearly two-thirds of the retailers who were approached sold tickets or cards to the under-age reporters and half of the retailers did not have the age limit clearly displayed. Camelot, the company which operates the National Lottery and its scratch cards, responded to this survey by saying that they took its results very seriously, had followed up each case and would continue to monitor the situation carefully.

This was good to hear. Less so were the frank reactions to using the scratch cards by the 12- to 15-year-old reporters who had bought them – none of them had tried the cards before and actually came back from their survey with winnings of £21. 'Sensational', 'wicked', 'pukka', 'a buzz', 'so tempting' were some of the comments. One 12-year-old girl said, 'I just want loads more now. If I had my way, I'd just buy ten and I'd just sit there and scratch them. If you spend £10 on this, you could win £25,000 – that's the whole point.'

The signs of compulsive gambling on scratch cards are very similar to the signs of addiction to fruit-machine gambling as listed above. One of the differences could be that more money is staked on cards, so that the child who is paying out non-stop on instants will be almost constantly borrowing money and failing to pay it back, lying about where it comes from, even stealing from friends and family. In fact, for the compulsive gambler of any age or type, friends and family become solely people from whom he can beg, borrow or steal – they have no other place in his life.

Steps to help the young gambler hooked on scratch cards will also be much the same as those hooked on fruit machines. That is to say that, once they're hooked, there's very little you can do to stop them. You and your addicted child will need help, certainly within the family and perhaps outside it too, as outlined in the next chapter.

Computers and video games

Ten years ago a psychiatrist in Glasgow was treating boys aged between 16 and 19 years who were using their home computers 12 hours a day. They had nightmares, illusions, excessive daydreaming and exhaustion, and one boy became psychotic. What was clear was that the state-of-the-art computer games were similar to those in arcade machines which are known to be addictive. So here was another risky area for children, another potential worry for parents.

In 1991, when the craze for these games was in full swing, sales of Nintendo, the home video games system, reached one million over the year. The most popular game for playing on the Nintendo console – *Super Mario Bros 3* – was selling just before Christmas at the rate of 1,000 an hour, and 600,000 of the console's hand-held little brother, *Gameboy*, had been sold in that year.

From America came reports of addicted *Gameboy*-owners laid low by exhaustion and damaged wrists; Nintendo was accused of corrupting youth worldwide; evangelical groups predicted family breakdowns. In the UK, Peter Dawson, head of the Professional Association of Teachers and a part-time lay preacher, warned parents of the signs of an addict: 'Lack of speech, little sign of life, total absence of thought.' He described *Gameboy* as 'A viable, cheaper alternative to brain surgery. It's a painless lobotomy at a fraction of the cost.'

The editor of the consumer magazine *What Toy?* had a more moderate view – 'We have had crazes before – remember turtles? In time, boredom will set in.' She was right. *Mario* and *Gameboy* have given way to ever more sophisticated games which have their brief period of popularity and give way to something else. The boredom factor still rules the market. In the last five years, perhaps partly because of the long-lingering recession, sales of video games, consoles, and home computer games have all declined but the sale of personal computers – not exclusively or even mainly for games playing, of course – continued with a steady rise, recently reaching a peak of over two million in the UK.

The attractions of computer-games playing for the young are:

- it takes place in their own home
- they don't have to pay
- it 'stretches time' – i.e. players can go on and on with no point at which it's appropriate to stop
- it's one of the few things in life over which they have control
- when their parents are computer-illiterate, games playing is a world they can't enter, let alone share
- success at playing can raise their self-esteem.

On the downside, research in America found that computer games were more and more biased towards aggression, sex and violence and fed directly into masculine fantasies of control, power and destruction. Alarm was being expressed in the UK about a possible link between computer/video games and aggressive behaviour. One expert concluded that the racist, sexist and violent content of computer games will, unless checked, have a serious impact not only on young people but on the whole of society.

A report by a group of teachers concluded that video- and computer-games playing can lead to:

- lack of concentration and perseverance
- aggression
- less reading and writing
- wrist, neck and elbow pain, epileptic seizures (not proven)
- isolation
- heavy spending (50 per cent of the children questioned spent £40-plus per month, 25 per cent said they would steal computer games if they had no money)
- lack of sports and exercise
- lack of friends and companions.

This is what can happen but how can we tell when our children are getting into the danger zone? To the rescue again comes Dr Mark Griffiths, the expert on fruit-machine gambling who has recently turned his attention to video and computer games as well. He has written a leaflet of advice for parents – 'Your Child and Video Games' (details in Chapter 12). Meanwhile, this is his check-list for parents who worry about the amount of time their children play video games and want to know 'How much is too much?'

- Do they play most days?
- Often play for long periods?
- Play for excitement?
- Get restless if they can't play?
- Play for a personal best?
- Often try unsuccessfully to limit playing?
- Play instead of doing homework?
- Sacrifice social activities?

If the answer is 'yes' to more than four questions, your children may be playing too much, says Dr Griffiths. You may have other worries besides the amount of time spent playing. What about the content of these games? What sort of effect are video games having on your children? Are they a risk to their physical or mental health? In the next chapter, 'Help for young gamblers', we'll look at the answers to these questions.

9
Help for young gamblers

The help a young gambler most needs – although he may not recognize it – is the back-up he gets within the family. Without this he may be unable to accept ultimately more useful help from people outside the family. If his family can't supply what he needs, then the outside people will have to do their best. I'm not talking about practical help here, which usually does have to come from outside the family, but answers to the youngster's emotional needs. To fix in our minds what those needs are, let's look at the factors in a youngster's personality which have been found to lead to compulsive gambling and see what they tell us:

- feeling inferior to peers and elders
- low self-esteem
- made to feel non-contributing
- feels it's important to win
- compulsive traits (in other areas as well as in gambling)
- early love of games of chance
- lack of responsibility for gambling
- first bet a win
- gambling offers personal status
- winning makes him feel like an achiever
- important to be the centre of attention
- gambling scene a substitute for parental affection.

This is undoubtedly a sad picture of someone who feels unloved, unwanted and useless, striving to be noticed, to climb higher in the pecking order, and to rate as a winner and an achiever, but more or less locked into his self-image as a completely unworthy, lowly all-out loser.

We learned, when looking at the reasons why adults become problem gamblers, that the common factor was lack of self-esteem or a very low self-image. We also learned that the problem gamblers themselves are likely to be unaware of this and wouldn't thank anyone who pointed it out. It's only when they are in the process of getting help, and begin to look at the inner man and what drives him, that they see the light and can recall feeling 'no good', or rejected or humiliated from an early age and embarking on a desperate search for approval and status.

It's the same for the young gambler – except that he may not ever come to know how he feels and why. That doesn't matter. What his family and helpers have to do is make him feel that, whatever happened in the past, he *is* loved now, he *does* count, he *can* be a somebody (only not by gambling) and he can confidently and responsibly rule his own life.

You, as his parent, might be saying – 'But hang on! He had a happy childhood. His Dad and I were always around for him. I didn't go out to work – I was always here when he came back from school. We weren't the lovey-dovey sort of family but he must have *known* we thought a lot of him. He was perfectly OK until he was 13 and started going to the arcades with some other boys . . . You can't blame us.'

Well, no one's blaming anyone. The difficulty is that it's not so much what a person's childhood was like in reality or as the parents see it that counts but how the child perceives it. He might have been loved this side of idolatry, well-nigh worshipped (although that would present other problems) but that would not make a jot of difference if the child did not actually *feel* loved, maybe because of the parent's faulty transmitter, maybe because of the child's faulty receiver – or maybe because, unknown to the parents themselves, they really didn't think much of the boy.

Whatever the reason, this bad feeling about oneself is what leads to all sorts of frantic strivings and addictions. Alcohol, drugs, sex, gambling, fame, and work can all be compulsively used in the search for status, approval and love. Your child might not have this bad feeling all the time or to any great extent but a little self-dislike goes a very long way and needs a disproportionate amount of loving approval to overcome it.

You might be convinced that your son doesn't have this bad feeling in any degree at all. In which case, all I'd say is that it won't do any *harm* to give him what he would be needing if he did feel he was a no-account no-hoper whom nobody cared for. What would he need if he did feel like that?

- Encouragement to find something he's good at it and go for it. Is he artistic, musical, sporty, mechanically minded, computer-literate? Find out what avenues there are for him to learn more about what interests him, doing some training, joining a class or a club. The local library and the local education authority have the information you'll need.
- Praise for any achievements, however small, that show a positive attitude to life or a sense of responsibility. If he does something off his own bat – even if it's not done quite the way you'd want it – show you appreciate it.
- Don't overdo the praise. He'll know when something he's done merits simply a 'Thank you – I'm pleased with the way you've done that.' If you go over the top – 'Oh, that's marvellous! You really are a

kind boy – what would I do without you?' – he'll latch on to the phoneyness and distrust all your expressions of approval or gratitude.

- He needs opportunities to contribute to the family or the running of the house. Give him some jobs for which he's entirely responsible – don't expect him to relish being second mate to your captain. Always give a warning about something that needs doing and give plenty of time for it to be done. Never, never interrupt what he's doing with the demand – 'I want this done *now*.'

- If he's earning any money at all, ask for a sum towards his keep, however small. Don't let it slide. 'If you're absolutely skint, I'll let you off this week' sounds like a kindness but it's not. It's extremely unhelpful because it knocks down one of the fixed boundaries that were keeping him inside his changed, new life. They may not be keeping him away from gambling yet but they are gradually building up an image of himself from which he doesn't have to try and escape.

- Whenever you can, look at him with pleasure and listen to him with understanding. It's easy to let these channels of communication get blocked without realizing it. In a lot of families, children and their parents simply don't look at each other much and if they look, they don't see. Similarly, we can let verbal communication fade away altogether. We don't listen much and when we listen we don't always hear. Even when we hear what's being said, we fail to round off the communication by showing we've heard.

All this may make it sound as if you're dealing with a very young child, one who is just starting out on the business of making relationships and finding his own place in the world and in the hearts of others. That is precisely what's happening. In dealing with a young problem gambler you are dealing with the vulnerable, uncertain child within, and the same applies to the adult problem gambler too. In every case, he is being asked to turn his whole life around, to start anew with a kind of rebirth, learning who he is, what he can do, what other people think of him.

This is, of course, something parents hope to do for their child in his actual early childhood – to help him acquire a firm sense of identity, self-respect and the knowledge that he's valued. So this programme for the young gambler's education in feelings rather than facts is, in effect, a blueprint for how to *prevent* a child ever being at risk of addiction to anything, and I will come back to this point at the end of this chapter.

Meanwhile, there's the problem of how best to help your young problem gambler through the practical steps of his recovery. There are very great difficulties – perhaps greater than the difficulties of coping with an adult gambler. An adolescent will often resent every attempt to help him, feeling that this truly reduces him to early childhood when he had no control over his own life. Unless he's getting help from a source specifically for gamblers, you can't reasonably expect him to give up gambling altogether and straight away. Few people, much less a youngster, can manage this without group support or help from outside the family. The main source of this practical help and support for young gamblers and their parents is the UK Forum on Young People and Gambling (full details are in Chapter 12). Here is some of their advice for parents:

- Remember you are not the only family facing this problem.
- If it's possible, talk things through with your child.
- If that doesn't work, see if someone else – teacher, another relative, a counsellor – can talk with him instead.
- Bear in mind that this is a serious problem and the gambler can't just 'give it up'.
- Take a firm stand. Don't give in to demands.
- Don't ever forget that a problem gambler is good at telling lies – to himself as well as to you. Don't believe all he says.
- Encourage him all the time towards change – though this may not happen until he's faced with a crisis.
- Let him take responsibility for the gambling and its consequences – if you take this on, he won't work at overcoming his dependency.
- Don't condemn – it could drive him back to gambling. It's more helpful to set fair and firm boundaries to his behaviour.
- Let him know that, despite all that's happened, you care about him. Do this even if you have to make a 'tough love' decision, like asking him to leave home.
- Don't trust him with money until he's free of his compulsion. If he agrees, manage his money for him for a while.
- Bear in mind that you, the parent, need support while you are going through the long process of helping your gambling child. You will certainly need this from the rest of the family and possibly from a helping agency as well. Details in Chapter 12.

If he won't let you near him, bide your time. Just 'be there' for when he's ready. At the same time, don't smother him. Respect his space and time, and expect him to respect yours. You know about 'tough love' – the kind of love which forces you to act harshly when it helps a child grow into maturity and independence. Love him toughly when you must, and tenderly too when it's appropriate.

Help from outside the family

Organized help for young gamblers and their parents started only about ten years ago in response to the worries about fruit-machine playing referred to in the last chapter. As always happens when there is a new, compelling need for support and help for a group in society who are disadvantaged or in danger, the challenge was met initially by enthusiastic and caring individuals off their own bat.

That's how Gamblers Anonymous started up in Britain and it's how the UK Forum on Young People and Gambling came into being. It's also how Parents of Young Gamblers started. These are the only organizations offering practical help specifically to gamblers, but there are other bodies working with parents which include gambling among the problems for which they offer initial help. I give details of all these organizations in Chapter 12.

Parents of Young Gamblers, run by Dave and Sue Jackson in Birmingham, was set up in 1986 when, Dave says, fruit machines were the main problem:

> There were 55 arcades in Birmingham when we started. Some of the kids playing were really young. These places don't turn money away – if you were big enough to reach the slot, you were in. A lot of the parents who came for help knew there was something wrong but thought their child was into drugs – some of them were euphoric when they found it was fruit machines. The main problem now is scratch cards. They're supposed to be for over-16s but they can get them at 14 or younger, no problem. They're very dangerous because they give an instant buzz.

Dave believes that the only cure is 'the talking cure', i.e. counselling. When a parent or child phones he gives them advice and information and tries to find a local source of help for one or both of them. He has no groups and no funds. His phone bills are enormous – often he is the only source of understanding and support for frantic parents. He gets no financial gain from helping young gamblers but says, 'I've never helped anyone before – I've surprised myself. But it's very rewarding.'

Incidentally, an interesting slant on the fruit-machine addict's behaviour and a novel suggestion for treatment is made by Mark Griffiths. He wanted to draw the attention of fruit-machine players to their irrational thinking during play. He used the 'thinking aloud' method with a group of 30 gamblers and recorded what the players said. Here's one player thinking out loud:

This fruity (fruit machine) is not in a good mood . . . Oh my, come on, *please* give me an orange . . . Well done! (*Thanks machine for giving him an orange*) . . . Did you see that? The machine snatched the win – bastard machine . . . it's really laughing at me here . . . Can I win more than 10p this time? *No!* . . . *Obviously this machine is being a bit of a bastard at the moment!*

Only four gamblers out of the 30 in the trial wanted to hear the play-back. None of the four could believe they'd said and thought what they did. However, one of them claimed that hearing the play-back stopped him gambling eventually.

This extract illustrates some of the factors consistently found in studies of fruit-machine gamblers – the way that regular players personify the machine, blame their losses on outside factors and attribute wins to their own skill. Mark Griffiths suggests that the thinking aloud method, by showing up these irrational thoughts to the player himself, might help to modify his behaviour. This seems to make sense – most therapies aim to replace irrationality with reason and to get there by enabling us to listen to ourselves. Even psychoanalysis, after all, is only a dressed-up version of the 'thinking aloud' method.

Can Gamblers Anonymous help young gamblers?

At one time GA's members were mostly over 20 and the majority were addicted to horse- and dog-racing and casino gaming. Now, however, the number of machine-gambling members is increasing slightly, though under-20s are still only a very small proportion of the members in most groups.

A workshop held by the UK Forum on Young People and Gambling discussed the possible reasons for young people's low take-up of GA's help and came up with the following list of suggested come-ons and turn-offs:

- *Come-ons*: The young gambler's desperation and fear. Legal pressure. Parent pressure. Parent attending GA. A way out of his financial crisis. Recognition of his problem. Friendly atmosphere. Learning about the destructive results of compulsive gambling.
- *Turn-offs*: Forced attendance. Lack of transport. Meetings clash with social life. Generation gap between members. Different form of gambling from older members. Different important life factors. Fear of unknown. Lack of relevant young literature. Can't relate to

emphasis on self-help. Meetings perceived as authoritarian. In a minority – may be only young person present.

To the question posed by the workshop – 'Is GA relevant to young gamblers?' – the answer turned out to be 'Sometimes'. However, the need is growing and GA groups are doing their best to respond to it. So, if you are a young gambler or the parent of one, it's well worthwhile approaching GA for help.

Worried about computer and video games?

Now we return to the question of computer- and video-games playing – in the last chapter you were left dangling on the question of how to cope with your worries about them.

Start by finding out exactly what's in the games your children play. You may be surprised to find that some of them, although sold as children's games, are quite unsuitable for your younger children and perhaps even on the borderline for adolescents. They may be graphically violent or show women in inferior roles or simply portray values you don't share and would rather your children didn't absorb.

If you do have some objections to the content of the games, or any other worry about them, that's a good reason to have a constructive discussion with your children about their games playing and, if necessary, make a few rules. Your aims should be:

- to help them choose suitable games that are still fun
- to talk with them about the content of games so that they understand the difference between make-believe and reality
- to discourage solitary games playing
- to guard against obsessive playing
- to follow recommendations on the possible risks: sit at least two feet from the screen; the room should be well-lit; never have the screen at maximum brightness; children should never play video games when they're tired.
- to ensure that your children have plenty of other interests to pursue in their free time besides playing video and computer games.

Prevention of problem gambling

It is significant that none of the organizations or individuals in the business of helping gamblers is anti-gambling. GA concedes that 'Gambling is fun for millions of people.' 'Our only concern,' says John, their spokesman, 'is the lack of knowledge given to the public by the gambling industry on what can happen if they spend more than they can afford.'

The UK Forum recognizes that it's an exciting form of entertainment which presents no problems when it's within the gambler's control. The Forum's aim is to prevent harm to young people through gambling, but in the present climate this is an uphill struggle and parents have to be more and more concerned about where their children are and what they're doing in their free time without becoming heavy-handed disciplinarians.

Opportunities to gamble in the UK are increasing all the time, and commentators are bandying phrases about like 'gambling fever' and 'the British disease'. Betting-shops are open seven days a week (they used to be closed on Sundays) and there is also horse-racing on previously banned Sundays. Football pools and fruit machines are more widely available, huge Lottery prizes are distributed every week and it seems that every newspaper and magazine, every company with something to sell, every firm that wants a come-on for customers are all running their own versions of scratch cards or the Lottery.

Both GA and the UK Forum on Young People and Gambling are perturbed that the age limit for playing on scratch cards and the Lottery is as low as 16. 'It's too easy to gamble now,' says John from GA, 'it's a temptation to young and old. People are looking for that dream – and they're going to suffer. Gambling is treated as a leisure-type thing when it's not – not for everyone. There aren't enough warnings or enough help for people who've gone OTT.' Paul Bellringer of the UK Forum describes scratch cards as 'hard gambling' and, in common with many other people, feels very strongly that the age limit on players should be raised to 18.

It doesn't look as if the problem is going to go away. The estimate for the number of compulsive gamblers in the UK is 100,000 under-18s and 1 million to 1.5 million adults. The view is that these numbers can only increase now that society has chosen to go down the road of easy, unfettered gambling. So there have to be restraints. Every society has a duty to watch over the vulnerable and disadvantaged and has to make potential dangers of different kinds – like fireworks, drugs, alcohol – less tempting and less accessible. For that duty to be fulfilled in relation to gambling, two things are needed: both education to prevent irresponsible gambling; and also funds for people who are helping and supporting problem gamblers.

On the issue of education, there really needs to be a major turn around in the kind of education for living that we at home, in schools and in society at large offer our children. There has to be something wrong with the present systems if the figures for alienation, crime, heavy drinking, compulsive gambling and the use of 'recreational' drugs among the young keep rising.

If you can't give a young man or woman the opportunity of a job, a home or creative input into society, at least you can give him or her the means to develop some other basis for self-esteem, a sense of belonging to a community and confidence in the future. Finding out how to do this needs a lot of research and money but, most of all, it needs a major shift in what we think is valuable and helpful for the young to know, especially those who are never going to make it to the pinnacles of what we laughingly call success, i.e. lots of money and lots of material goodies.

Personally, I think it's vital for the young to learn all about how to survive with their integrity intact and how to protect themselves and those who may depend on them against the contemporary dangers arising from greed, aggression and insecurity. They need to know how to find satisfaction and joy in relationships rather than in possessions, how to develop an interest in creative pursuits and how to live cooperatively instead of competitively.

This isn't a tall order. It would be enough to bring it about if education did what it seldom does, and if parents did what they've had little opportunity to learn to do, which is give all young people the means and the confidence to be the best they can be, as themselves and in whatever roles they choose to take on, and to think well enough of themselves – and with good reason – not to *need* escapes into violence or addictions or emotional detachment.

Prevention also means helping children to know all about the background to gambling, just as they're told about alcohol and drugs and where the dangers begin. This need for education has been summed up by Paul Bellringer, of the UK Forum, in a letter to a newspaper: 'Children should be prepared for this adult activity through education programmes linked to the national curriculum so that they can make an informed choice and develop a responsible approach to gambling. A comprehensive programme is urgently needed and we believe it is appropriate if this be financed by money generated from gambling.'

10
Help for parents

How do you cope with the suspicion or the certainty that your child is addicted to gambling? Another parent may have told you about his reputation among the other kids as a gambler who can't stop. This is merely a suspicion. Or there may be no doubt that something's very wrong. Perhaps the police are involved. Gambling is not a crime but, as we've seen, it can lead to crime and your child might have been caught shoplifting or stealing. Perhaps you've learnt that he's been playing truant and the school or the education authority is involved. Even if you have all this evidence of deep trouble, you still can't be sure what the trouble is. This has to come from him. Incidentally, once more I'm talking about *his* problem and how you cope with *him* but in this context everything I say about coping with a gambling son applies to the far less likely case of a gambling daughter.

So, whether it's suspicion or fact the first thing is to have a talk with him. You could hinder the process of getting at the truth by approaching this talk in the wrong way, especially if it's aggressive. Here is the way that's been found to work best.

- Don't pitch straight in as soon as you've had a hint of the trouble. Talk with your partner or a trusted friend first – just to get things into perspective. Don't try to work out what line you're going to take and what you intend to do about the problem – wait till you have the whole picture.
- Choose an open-ended time when neither you nor your child has to dash off anywhere. Try to make it a time free of interruptions. Be prepared for the discussion to last quite a while. Never mind all the pauses. Just stick at it calmly until you feel satisfied that you have the full picture and he shows signs of having understood that the crunch has come and something is going to be done about it.
- Don't start with an accusation – 'You've been seen in the arcade several mornings this week – don't deny it.' He will deny it. He's been denying his gambling and truanting for months and got away with it. Start with a question that invites him to tell you what's wrong. Say that you're worried – 'You haven't been yourself for ages. Can you tell me what's wrong?' or 'I've heard that lots of teenagers are going mad on scratch cards – have you ever tried them?'

94

- Let him have his say. Never mind if he starts with excuses and justifications – you don't have to believe them and you don't have to stamp on them either. You must expect him to defend his corner right up until the time when he has to accept that this is the end of the road and change starts here.
- Don't let him make light of the problem. He has to know that it's serious. Equally he has to know that you are not expecting a lightning transformation from gambler to non-gambler. It will take time, tell him, and you might not, in the end, even be asking him to give up gambling entirely. He might be able to control his gambling to a sensible level he can afford. That will be up to him.
- Let him know that you are on his side.
- Don't assume that gambling is the whole problem. There's probably some other worry that made him turn to gambling in the first place – depression, loneliness, chronic lack of confidence, bullying, fear of failure at school or conflicts within the family. Tell him that whatever troubles him, he can be helped, if only by letting it all see the light. You can't promise remedies but you can promise understanding and some ideas for lightening his load.
- Tell him that nothing's going to be done, no step taken without his knowledge. If it has his agreement fine; if not, too bad.
- If he can't or won't open up first time round, have another talk a few days later. If he still clams up, ask him if he'd prefer to talk to someone outside the family, and have sources of help ready – see Chapter 12.

You're going to be doing a lot of listening to your child's feelings. What about yours? This crisis may be the first serious one concerning your children that you've had to tackle. It often seems that our law-abiding, open-faced 14-year-olds turn into glowering, moody, tongue-tied hermits overnight and that, just when you need them, all the former channels of communication are tightly closed. Don't despair. The 14-year-old, and indeed, the one-year-old, the five-year-old and the ten-year-old are all there underneath. In fact, it is how family life was in those years, while he was growing up, that will partly determine how this crisis is going to be resolved. Those earlier years of family life are also the key to safeguarding our children against the dangers lying in wait for them, including the risk of some form of addiction – more of that later.

Parents' feelings

For now, we're looking at the impact of your child's problem on you. Here are some of the reactions and feelings you're likely to have and how to deal with them.

Panic

A panic reaction is understandable but unnecessary. Take a deep breath and calm down. A gambling addiction is not life-threatening unless the addict has no help and no support. It isn't even a health threat unless the addict is completely on his own and doesn't look after himself. Remember that you're far from alone with your problem – thousands of other families throughout the country are tackling it too. Just make the decision that you're going to be one of the families who deal with it as calmly and sensibly as you can.

Blaming yourself

I guess it's a sign of most parents' lack of confidence nowadays but the first reaction of responsible parents to the news that their child is in real trouble is 'What did we do wrong?' Unfortunately, there are also a lot of parents in the same situation who react with 'Well, it's not because of anything we've done or not done. It must be the people he mixes with/ the television/the lack of discipline at school . . .'

These parents need to know that, whatever the influences from outside that bombard children, the home is where these influences are filtered through the family's values, sorted into positive and negative and either absorbed or discarded. However, some influences and temptations are so powerful that they slip through the net and whisk a child off to experimental, exciting pleasures with the potential for addiction.

This happens even more easily when there's no values-net at all in the family but I still wouldn't say that the family is wholly to blame for that. Most of us get no help in learning how to be parents or how to equip our children to survive in a fragmented, stressful society. We're much more likely to get thumped for failing.

Confusion

This arises out of the big question 'How did it happen?' The early days after discovering the problem is not the best time to ask this question. Better to deal with the immediate needs first – for help and support, information, cooperation with the police and school if they're involved, etc. – and put the idea of a sort-out to the back of your mind until you can approach it in a relaxed way.

Anxiety

Naturally, you'll be worried about your child, wondering if he'll ever recover from his compulsive gambling and what his future will be, how the family's going to cope, will your partner support you, will the other children be harmed? It's easy to be so paralysed and overwhelmed by worries like this that you're quite unable to think straight or do anything to deal with the worries.

You can overcome this paralysis in the following ways:

- By developing some regular form of relaxation and exercise. The pressures and insecurities of modern living make the ability to relax essential for most people, even when life is rushing along fairly smoothly. This ability to switch off from our worries and take the long view is needed even more in a crisis. Going over the top emotionally or sinking under the weight of stress is going to make the problem very much harder to deal with.

- If you feel badly depressed, get help from your doctor. Don't be worried about having medication if necessary – it's only a temporary crutch until you're back to normal.

- Don't bottle up your problems. If you don't share them, you'll suffer much more. If you have an understanding partner, talk things through together – but not all day and every day. If your partner is the father of the child in trouble, you can expect as much input from him as from yourself – with understanding and constructive interest if not with time. Let him know how much he's needed – by you and the child.

- If your partner is a step-parent, I think you should still expect him to share your worries to the full, if not for the child's sake, then for yours. If he can only offer condemnation of the child and impatience with you, don't confide in him and keep the child out of his way, if possible. Then get help for yourself, starting with the UK Forum on Young People and Gambling.

- If things continue to buzz round in your head, get all the events, information, advice and worries about the crisis down on paper. A sort of diary can be very useful in an ongoing crisis. In it you put, for example, appointments for you or the child with social worker, counsellor, Citizens Advice Bureau, doctor, the courts, solicitor and, after these meetings, what decisions were made and what actions, if any, have to be taken. You can note down steps back and steps forward, when he apparently nipped out for a gamble, for instance, and when he voluntarily told you about it. It will all help you to see you're getting somewhere.

Shame

One thing I learned from my years as an agony aunt is how terribly ashamed a lot of people are when they're in need of help. Even when things have gone wrong through no conceivable fault of theirs they speak of their shame well before they tell you what the problem is. So this is something you have to guard against. You certainly don't need any emotion that's going to shove you down any further than you already are. Talk about it freely with friends and neighbours if you want to. Don't if you don't. Be proud that you're facing up to the problem and doing something about it. Hold your head high and your son will get the message that while he is actively trying to overcome his problems he has no reason to slink around like a criminal.

Anger

Your anger at your child's behaviour is taken for granted. It's how you handle it that counts, and that depends on how you've been used to dealing with anger all your life and how your whole family has been used to dealing with it. Everyone knows that we don't get rid of anger by not expressing it. All we do is push it out of sight where it festers away and spreads its poison all through our relationships with people.

So anger is best let out – but not any old how and at full volume. The first step is to be honest and say you're angry. He has to know that he has stepped over the limits of your tolerance and that you care enough for his welfare to be riled that he's put it at risk. You can say how angry you are as strongly as you like – 'I'm *furious*, I don't know when I've ever been so angry, I feel like smashing all those damn fruit machines' – but what you must try not to do is make a verbal assault on the child himself or his character – 'You're just hopeless', 'You're a dreadful disappointment to us', 'You're no good', etc. You have to make it clear that your anger is against the song, not the singer.

Sorrow

It's always rather sad when our children pass some milestone or other and move on to a different phase in their lives. The first major spot of trouble concerning a child is no less a rite of passage than his first day at school. You are, in both cases, a little sad to have lost the child he was. In the case of uncovering an addiction, you are even more sad that what previously seemed like a comparatively carefree, trusting boy around the house, making noise and nuisance, has suddenly turned into this withdrawn figure, half-defiant, half-shamefaced, who is having to come to terms with the temptations and dangers of adult life.

Perhaps this bit of sadness is an asset in a way. It can help you to see the confused child behind the closed shutters. It can rouse your compassion and put you on his side. You can recognize it, make use of it and then take it in your stride. Mothers are mostly terrific softies and can feel pangs of sadness at almost anything – they sob at weddings and even have a little weep at happy endings in advertisements. So weep away if you feel like it. Tears are always better shed than dammed back.

Loneliness

If you're a single parent, a crisis like this can be a very big burden to bear alone. It's not necessarily, however, any bigger than the load a parent bears whose partner is indifferent to the children or even hostile to them when there's any trouble about their behaviour. In either of these cases, one hopes that you would have built up a network of friends, probably among other parents, and have access to some source of advice, information and support for parents. See Chapter 12.

When you feel really low – or even just in need of a friendly listening ear – don't forget that the Samaritans are on the end of the phone 24 hours a day to help anyone through any worry or patch of despair.

Guarding against gambling

Whether you're reading this book because you have a youngster in the family who's into gambling or because you want to be prepared in case this is a problem that lies ahead of you, you're probably wondering if there's anything you can do to guard against your children ever becoming addicted. Well, there's certainly a way of being a parent that makes it very much less likely that your children will want to escape into drug-taking, gambling, heavy drinking or any dangerous or antisocial behaviour, but it's not a response to a crisis, it's a way of family life.

This way starts almost as soon as the child is born and continues throughout its life. It's based primarily – you've guessed it – on nurturing the child's self-esteem. It also fosters his sense of security, self-confidence and, later, his independence. These are the things, as we have found out in previous chapters, that the addicts, the isolated, the losers and loners are short of. This is not to say that your way of bringing up your children has been or is wrong, harmful or no good. It's merely saying that, unless it has most of the features of the approach I'm going to outline, it's not such a good safeguard against the dangers today's children are up against.

Keep the channels of communication open between all members of the family. Talk through your worries with each other – either one-to-one when appropriate or in round-the-table family discussions.

Encourage the expression of feelings from an early age. Don't ever let a child think his anger, his sadness or any other feeling is unacceptable. Always let *him* tell you how he feels; don't *you* ever tell him how he feels. If you think that sounds obvious, just think about how often you've heard the following exchange or something like it:

MOTHER:'What's wrong? You look down in the dumps.'
CHILD: 'I wish Kevin wasn't coming to play.'
MOTHER:'That's nothing to be mopey about! You know you like him –
        he's your best friend. Come on, give us a smile. Look cheerful
        or he won't want to come again.'

The lesson here is that it's wrong to have any feelings of your own. Mother wants you to feel the way she does about everything – including rotten Kevin who pinches you all the time and won't play anything unless he can win. She's saying that you're wrong to dislike Kevin. What you should do is go about all the time with a phoney smile on your face, pretending that nothing upsets you or makes you angry. Thus develops the repressed, cowed, vulnerable child who feels unreal and unacceptable – and who will be on the look-out for any escape from these painful feelings.

What would be a better way of handling this situation?

MOTHER:'What's wrong? You look down in the dumps.'
CHILD: 'I wish Kevin wasn't coming to play.'
MOTHER:'Why's that? Isn't he your best friend any more?'
CHILD: 'He certainly isn't. I hate him.'
MOTHER:'What's he done to make you feel like that?'
CHILD: 'He pinches. And he doesn't play fair.'
MOTHER:'That sounds horrid. Would you rather he didn't come to
        play?'
CHILD: 'Wonderful! Can you stop him coming today?'
MOTHER:'No, that wouldn't be kind. Do your best to get on with him
        today and we'll have a talk afterwards to see how you feel
        about him coming again or not.'

Talk openly with your children about life's problem areas – smoking, drugs, sex, violence, different forms of abuse, and do it when they first ask questions about the subject – but make your responses appropriate to the child's age and understanding. Don't lay down the law. Start by asking them what they think about the problem. Have they come across anyone who takes drugs, say? Do any of their friends smoke? What do they think about abortion? There shouldn't be any subject that can't be discussed in the family. Then, if trouble strikes, you have a headstart on communicating about the facts and feelings of that particular problem.

Expect the best of your children until proved wrong. If you always expect the worst – 'I don't suppose you remembered to post my letter,' 'Did you pinch my pen? Come on, give it back', 'Well, all right, you can switch to chemistry if you want – but you'll find it much too hard' – you're handing your child tremendous put-downs that will not only lower his self-confidence but also give him absolutely nothing to live up to. Expecting the best will do the opposite by encouraging him to live up to your good opinion of him.

Don't try to shield your children from disappointments, frustration, conflict or pain. These are all part of real life – and real life is what we all have to live. Instead, help them face up to reality – talk together about their negative experiences and support them through them. Afterwards, they will have learnt a valuable lesson – that challenges and problems can be positive experiences. They don't destroy you – which is the horror they expect if you constantly shield them from these experiences – and, best of all, they grow in confidence and independence with each difficulty overcome.

Set firm and reasonable limits to their forays into the outside world. When they reach the age of going out with friends and without you, give them a set of rules – presented as 'because it saves me worrying unnecessarily' and not as a matter of discipline – so that you'll know where they are, who they're with and what time they'll be back. You don't need to know what they actually do every minute they're out. 'Did you have a good time?' is enough to evoke whatever they choose to tell you about their outing, including any worries they may have. Firm boundaries establish a sense of security, trust and something to grow out of into independence. Provided they stick to these limits, trust them. As they grow older, adapt the rules to each individual child's level of maturity and independence.

Get to know their friends and their friends' parents and make them welcome in your home. Start this when they're at primary school and keep it up at least until their adolescence. Having a teenage gang within earshot is not everyone's idea of a good time but it spares you the worries about where they are and who they're mixing with.

When you have this framework of communication, trust and understanding in place in the family, you'll be able to feel much more confident that your child will not be drawn into an addiction (he won't *need* it), and, if he is, that he'll be well-equipped, with help, to handle it and get free of it.

11
Safe gambling – your choice

We've talked about how you can help and get help when other members of the family have gambling problems – how about your problems? If you gamble at all you're bound sometimes to wonder if it's wrong or too much or if you're getting hooked. Because of the moralistic background to gambling in the UK, most of us tend to have a guilty feeling about the simple act of placing a bet.

When I see friends in the queue for lottery tickets or scratch cards at the local newsagents and say, 'Hullo' they immediately get that 'caught in the act' look. They shuffle their feet a bit and launch on some kind of explanation for their 'wrongdoing' – 'I only spend £2', 'It's not for me, of course, it's for John – he's the gambler in the family', or 'Whoops! You've caught me – the only time I've ever gone in for the Lottery.' (This is a real dud – what is she going to say when I see her in the queue again next week?)

Well, I'd like you to feel happy about gambling. It would be a good thing if everyone who gambled had no guilty feelings about it and felt that what they were doing was not endangering their well-being or mental health and certainly not bringing the family or the country to its knees. One of the worries that people have about gambling is the same as the worries we have about eating, drinking, smoking and sex – 'Am I overdoing it?', 'Is the amount that I eat/drink/smoke/make love too much?'

The answer to these questions depends on a definition of 'too much'. This has to be *your* definition, no one else's. The amount and frequency of any activity of yours is your responsibility and has to fit in with your circumstances, nature and needs. One of these needs, which is almost universal and which most people bear in mind when making decisions about what they do and how much they do it, is the desire not to hurt others. So this might come into your thinking about what is 'too much'.

Generally speaking, 'too much' of something is when you feel fed up and cross with yourself for doing it as much as you do. 'Too much' is when you feel you ought to do less, or really want to, but fail to cut down. It's the way you feel when you're on a diet and you fall for a doughnut or a bag of chips. Or when you have a bout of chain-smoking when you were trying to limit yourself to one cigarette an hour. You feel ashamed and unworthy. You might even feel so bad that you give yourself a temporary boost with 'What the heck – this isn't my bag anyway . . .' and totally chuck in the attempt to cut down. And that ends by making you feel more guilty and fed up than you did before, so the uphill climb, if it continues at all, will be starting from an even lower rung and will be that much harder.

However, feelings about gambling are seldom as cut-and-dried as feelings about going over the top with any other activity. Fears about gambling 'too much' are usually vague doubts about whether one's spending too much, spending money which would be better spent on other things, or wasting one's money. With those gambling activities, like the Lottery, which have been monstrously hyped, a lot of people worry that they are so easily being seduced into parting with their money. Unfortunately, these worries don't go away. The more that gambling becomes an issue in the papers, on television and in Parliament, the more involved we become in the debate and the more important it is that each of us individually decides where we stand on the matter of our own gambling and on the gambling scene as a whole.

Another reason for dealing with any doubts or guilt feelings we may have about gambling is that feeling guilty is a real downer and can only be ended by stopping what makes you feel guilty or modifying it until you feel comfortable with it. Stopping the activity – gambling or anything else – makes no sense if you have a good reason for doing it. So why not instead modify it a little – cut down the frequency or the amount you stake, or switch to a form of gambling, or some other activity, that better answers your needs and doesn't make you feel guilty?

The first step in this process is to ask yourself 'Why am I gambling? What's making me buy this ticket, fill in this pools coupon or place this bet?' The main reason is simply that, as we learned in Chapter 1, the gambling instinct is in our bones and we like to take a chance on benefiting from making a bet. But when it comes to acting on this instinct, why do we do it?

Why do you gamble?

- For a bit of fun.
- Because your family and friends do.
- To get some money for the little extras of life.
- To get some money to make ends meet.
- To pay off your debts.
- To pay for some really big things you want, e.g. a new car, a cruise.
- To get enough money to turn your whole life around.

- To get money to help relations and friends solve their problems.
- To contribute to charity.
- To give you something to look forward to.
- To give you some company (when playing in a syndicate or a club).
- Because you'd feel 'left out' if you didn't gamble at all.
- Because it's nice thinking what you'd do with a big win and if you don't play, you'll never win.
- To give you the only spot of excitement in your life.

The harsh fact is that the first of these reasons is the only good reason for gambling. Gambling is a branch of the entertainment business and you take part in it to be entertained. It's not a way of getting hold of some money. On the contrary, apart from the remote chance of a very large win, it's primarily a way for you to lose money. When it comes to big losses, overindulging and feeling guilty, then you're not being entertained at all – the fun bit has gone – and you're spending big bucks to be made miserable and to make the gambling operators happy.

What about the other reasons for gambling? I'm not saying that they, in contrast with the first reason, are *bad* reasons, only that they aren't valid, they don't stand up, they don't actually do what you think they do or they are not as effective in meeting your need as some other activity would be. Some of them are more likely than others to lead you into problem gambling. Let's examine them more closely.

Because your family and friends do

Doing what everyone around you does is a strange way of carrying on, when you really think about it. Would you dye your hair red if they did, join the Moonies, become a vegetarian? Of course you wouldn't. You're master of your own fate. You'd do these things because you wanted to or not at all.

So if this is your reason, think again. Either recognize the fact that you gamble because you want to and you enjoy it, or face up to the possibility that you're a sheep that follows the herd and would be in danger of overdoing things if that's what they did.

To get some money for the little extras of life

It's a well-known fact that, unless you're a professional gambler, you can never emerge a winner over a long period of time. Therefore, overall, you are a loser, even if you have a few wins. The money you stake and lose would probably have paid for those little extras. So why not keep this money for yourself instead of donating it to the bookies and gambling operators?

To pay off your debts

Another well-known fact about any type of gambling is that it doesn't repay your debts, it adds to them. The best way of repaying debts is to get some debt counselling – your local Citizens Advice Bureau can help or put you on to someone who can – and make arrangements with all your creditors to pay back small, regular amounts. If you don't, the debts will go on growing and no amount of gambling can give you the reality or the hope of ending them. Never, never, say the experts, take out another loan to pay off previous loans and other debts. It's a way into disaster, not a way out of debt.

It's interesting to note that when some people do get hold of a lump sum to pay off their debts, it's not long before they are back where they started with about the same amount of indebtedness. It's almost as if in financial matters we find our own level, like water. On the whole, the solvency level seems best but some people feel quite comfortable with credit and debts as ongoing facts of life. If no one else is harmed, good luck to them.

To get some money to make ends meet

What you are asking for here is some more income. You want a regular sum to put into your budget to cover your day-to-day personal and household expenses. Well, that can't come from gambling. There's nothing regular or reliable, or even likely, about funds from that source.

Again, you're wasting your stake money. It would be better spent on a class or training course on something that would enable you to earn some extra money. Or there might be some part-time work you could do in your neighbourhood, or some paid work at home (look in the local paper). Start to pin your hopes on what *you* can do instead of what gambling might do for you. The chances are that it won't do a thing for you whereas you can do almost anything if you put your mind to it.

To pay for some really big things you want

The saddest thing about the Lottery's gigantic prizes and high profile is that they have made people believe that the material goodies they dream about are only round the corner – that it's only a matter of time before you too are posing for the cameras with the champagne bottle and the mile-wide grin on your face. As one lottery player said gleefully: 'It's marvellous! I'm not playing for a holiday on a Pacific island. Blow that! I'm playing for the whole island!'

This is not the effect that other forms of gambling have had. No one has ever made a dash for the casino or the bookie's office with the conviction that this visit is going to bring them that car or that cruise they pine for. Even the football pools, with some of their top wins up to the two million mark, never put the punters into such a lather that they killed themselves because the coupon didn't go in at the right time. Neither, pre-Lottery, was there anything like the unsavoury quarrels between winners and their families about the division of the loot. It seems to be all the result of hopes raised so high that, when they crash for whatever reason, the disappointment is unendurable for some and makes others seethe with envy.

No one can do anything about the effect of this hype – though a lot less of it would be a very good thing – but we can lessen its effect on us. We can look at our hopes in a rational way and reduce them to manageable proportions. We can be cynical about the ways big business tries to take our money off us – and cynical too about how the government gets us to pay more taxes and to contribute more of our private resources to items of public expenditure which are their responsibility.

The result of thinking this over could make you trim your dreams to something you might be able to afford in time. Or it might leave you with a dream you still hope will be fulfilled one day, in which case it might be better to use a form of gambling that gives you more than a 14.5 million to one chance of attaining it. As I noted elsewhere, these lottery odds are the worst ever in the history of gambling and the argument that 'someone's got to win' doesn't make them any better.

There's one thing about 'the big dream' that's always cheered me. I've often noticed that people who hope and strive for years for something they badly want go completely to pieces when they finally get it. Sometimes it was less than they had expected, sometimes it was more than they could handle, sometimes it was simply not as wonderful as they had imagined from a distance. Often a marriage that had been strong whilst working towards the dream fell apart when it became real. A dream come true can sometimes end in a life gone awry. The most comforting thing of all to those of us who dream beyond our reach is something one of Shaw's characters said in *Heartbreak House* – 'There are two tragedies in life. One is not to get your heart's desire. The other is to get it.'

To win enough money to turn your whole life around

This reason for gambling really only applies to the Lottery, where the jackpot is always several millions of pounds and certainly big enough to turn your whole family's life around. It's actually rather a sad reason for gambling – natural, universal and understandable, but still sad. A psychologist has pointed out that the desire to be taken right out of our everyday world – 'The grotty week', he called it – into a completely different environment and way of life is a terrible indictment of the quality of life most of us have.

Of course, a lot of people did have a terrible life before the Lottery and still do, but my feeling is that there are thousands and thousands more people who long to change their lives because there's now a remote chance that they could afford to do so. I wonder how many people who could say, before the Lottery, that they were quite content with life as it is, would say the same after the Lottery had been running for a few months? Not many, I bet. We're now conditioned to scratch at our discontents – and they simply don't heal.

This isn't an argument for not having the mega-fantasies that transport us into another world. Better to have them and enjoy them than not have any fantasies at all. What it's sensible to guard against is the idea that, because the fantasy is so huge and the odds against realizing it equally enormous, you're in no danger of getting completely hooked on the attempt. The Lottery drew a lot of people into the gambling scene who didn't at first think of themselves as gamblers. Now, however, they know they've substantially added to the number of real gamblers in the country. Any danger in that? There certainly is. As all the experts point out, the more gamblers you have, the more problem gamblers you get.

To get money to help relations and friends solve their problems

This is nice of you but there aren't many problems that can be solved by having money thrown at them. Illness, bereavement, divorce, handicap, loneliness, depression, rejection, love lost or never found, loss of a friend, a pet, a job, a hope – these are the sort of problems for which people turn for help to their relations and friends, and sometimes to agony aunts. What they need is your time, concern, company, listening, and sympathy, the cup of tea, the touch of a hand, the arm round the shoulders, the hug and the details of an on-the-spot source of practical help. You could give them all that without a trip to the betting-shop.

To contribute to charity

The Lottery donates part of its profits to charity, and so do many pools firms, smaller lotteries and 'instants' operators. They all emphasize that by gambling in this way you are helping good causes. You are – but not as generously as you perhaps thought. The fact is that of every £1 you spend on the Lottery, 28 pence is left for 'good causes' after overheads, taxes, profits and prize money have been extracted. Of that 28p, 5.6p goes to charity, making this one of the least effective and least bountiful ways of giving.

However, in the first year of the Lottery's operation, there were cries of anguish from many charities who said that contributions from the public had taken a tumble, from medical charities who were given a low priority for lottery money and from deserving causes who had been found undeserving in the first share-out. Fund-raisers of all kinds said that takings were down – 10 per cent fewer people were donating via raffles, lotteries, etc., and 4 per cent fewer were putting money in the charity street-collector's tins. A cancer charity called Tenovus reported a loss of 1.5 million (projected to the annual rate) since the Lottery started.

If, therefore, your main reason for gambling is to benefit a good cause, you'd be wiser to forget the gambling and make a direct donation to the charity of your choice.

To give you something to look forward to

This is an OK reason to gamble because it's exciting to anticipate the pleasure of gambling and the joy of a win, even if the glow fades immediately after the result. The danger is when gambling is the *only* thing in your life to look forward to. If there's nothing and no one else to give you a buzz or provide moments of stimulation and pleasure, then you're on dangerous ground and heading for addiction. Share your enthusiasm among a good range of objects and it will never get out of control.

To give you some company

Bingo clubs and casinos are companionable forms of gambling and betting-shops are looking up in that direction too – some of them serve drinks and snacks. Doing the pools or the Lottery in a syndicate is another sociable way of gambling, and all these group activities are probably some safeguard against going over the top. One of the characteristics of the budding addict is the preference for gambling alone. Again, however, it would be a pity if gambling were your only form of social life. If it alternated with a different kind of outing or a course of study or some community project, you'd be getting a good mix of social activities and not unwisely staking all on the gambling.

Because you'd feel left out if you didn't gamble at all

It's certainly quite nasty being the only one in a crowd who doesn't do something that all the rest do and not being able to join in the talk about it. Although there's no future in forcing yourself to join in something you really don't like, it's always worth trying it at least once if your friends enjoy it and would like you to be with them.

What you want to avoid is taking the same stance as a few people in the earlier years of television who stood out against having a set at all while neighbours and children's friends were chattering all the time about last night's good programme and asking 'Did you see. . . ?' After a while, doing without a television set became a matter of pride and prejudice rather than a rational choice. Don't let anything like that influence your decision to gamble or not to gamble.

If you do decide in the end that gambling's not for you, then don't join in but just remember that it's your choice – there's no reason to feel 'left out' if you've opted out. You could also look around for opportunities to join a crowd that was more to your taste.

Because it's nice thinking what you'd do with a big win and if you don't play, you'll never win

This is true. I can't think of any argument against it as a reason for gambling. It answers the desire for profit, the fantasy game and the buzz. Have fun.

To give you some excitement

The same applies here as to the social life and the anticipation experience – don't let gambling be your only outlet for either of these.

What's 'safe' gambling?

The main difference between the safe and dangerous gambler is that the safe kind goes about the activity responsibly and the dangerous kind doesn't. So what should you do if you want to be a safe, responsible gambler?

- Keep your gambling money completely separate from household money, loan repayments, family expenses, etc.
- Never look on your gambling as a source of income or a way of getting out of debt. Remember that you're buying a slice of entertainment, nothing more.

- Only use an amount of money that you don't mind losing.
- Every time you gamble decide exactly how much money you can afford to spend – like you would on a shopping trip – and don't go over it.
- If a win gets you some extra money, don't stake all of it on another chance – keep some of it back for next time. In other words, stop gambling while you're ahead.
- Watch that gambling isn't taking up a lot of your free time. Make sure you have other interests.
- If you find yourself wanting to gamble more and more or getting badly rattled when you can't gamble, pause for a review of the situation. See if you can cut down and calm down of your own accord. If not, ring Gamblers Anonymous.

12

Sources of help and information

Organizations

UK Forum on Young People and Gambling
(incorporating electronic game playing by young people)

PO Box 5, Chichester, West Sussex PO19 3RB
Tel: 01243 538635

The national centre for information, advice and practical help over the whole range of gambling activities followed by young people in the UK. Enquiry line open during office hours on weekdays for young problem gamblers and any family member. Newsletters, list of publications, advice leaflets, e.g. 'Signs, Symptoms, Stresses of Gambling Dependency', 'Young Gambling: A Guide for Parents' including the leaflet mentioned in Chapter 8 – 'Your Child and Video Games: Advice to Parents' by Dr Mark Griffiths (free but send an A4 sae).

Parents of Young Gamblers

Tel: 0121 443 2609

Advice and information, mainly relating to the Birmingham area, for parents of young gamblers – and the gamblers themselves if needed.

Gamblers Anonymous (GA)

PO Box 88, London SW10 0EU
National helpline: 0171 384 3040

GA has around 200 self-help groups throughout the country which hold regular meetings for the mutual support and encouragement of men and women who are trying to break their gambling habit. For details of your nearest group, ring or write (enclosing an sae).

Gam-Anon

Address and telephone number the same as for GA

GA's 'sister' organization which holds separate meetings for partners, friends and family of problem gamblers, providing support and advice on motivating a gambling partner or friend to go for help.

Youth Access

Magazine Business Centre, 11 Newarke Street, Leicester LE1 5SS
Tel: 01509 210420

Represents over 200 agencies nationally involved in providing information, advice and counselling to young people. Ring Youth Access for details of your nearest help centre.

Exploring Parenthood

4 Ivory Place, 20a Treadgold Street, London W11 4BP
Advice line and call-back service: 0171 221 6681
General enquiries: 0171 221 4471

Information and workshops for parents exploring the issues of parenthood. Send an sae for a publications list or call the advice line which is open to non-members.

Parent Network

44–46 Caversham Road, Kentish Town, London NW5 2DS
Tel: 0171 485 8535

Network of local parent support groups to help parents and children cope with the everyday problems of family life.

Parentline

Tel: 01268 75077

Support groups throughout the country for parents with worries about children of all ages. Ring for details of your local group.

National Council for One Parent Families

255 Kentish Town Road, London NW5 2LX
Tel: 0171 267 1361

The British Association for Counselling

1 Regent Place, Rugby CV21 2PJ
Tel: 01788 578328

Send an A5 sae for information on BAC publications and details of local counselling agencies and individual counsellors.

Further reading

Gordon Moody MBE, *Compulsive Gambling*, Thorsons, 1990
  This is out of print but is worth asking for at your local library.
David Spanier, *Easy Money: Inside the Gambler's Mind*, Oldcastle Books, 1995
  A selected list of publications held by the UK Forum on Young People and Gambling is available free for an A4 stamped, self-addressed envelope from the Forum's address as above.

Index